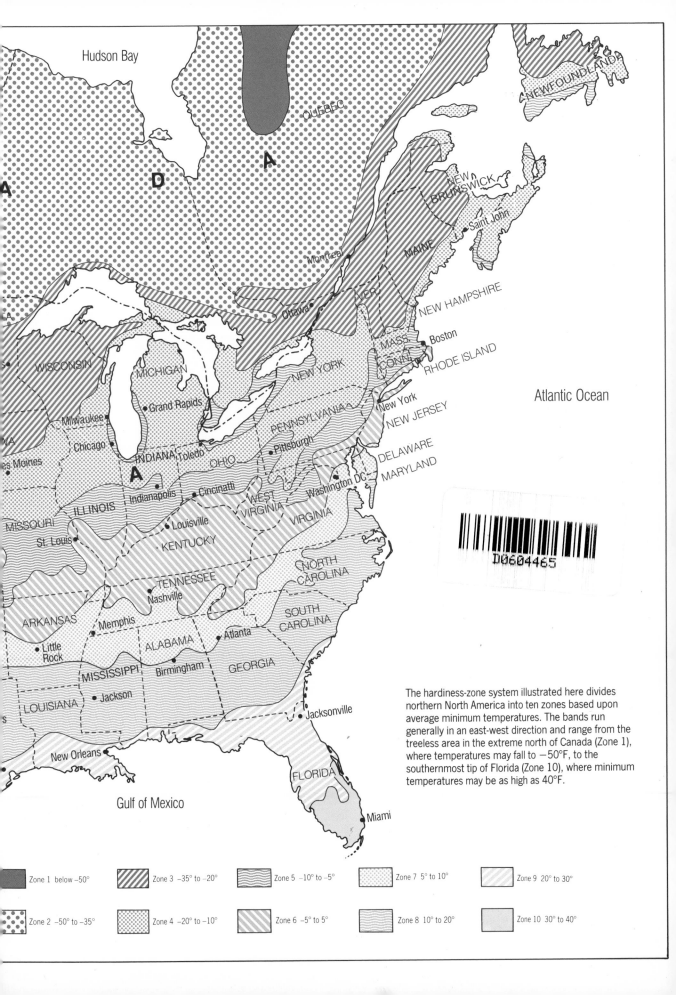

Hudson Bay

QUEBEC

NEWFOUNDLAND

A

D

NEW BRUNSWICK

Saint John

MAINE

Montreal

Ottawa

NEW HAMPSHIRE

Boston

MASS.

CONN.

RHODE ISLAND

Atlantic Ocean

WISCONSIN

MICHIGAN

NEW YORK

Grand Rapids

PENNSYLVANIA

New York

NEW JERSEY

Milwaukee

Chicago

INDIANA

Toledo

OHIO

Pittsburgh

DELAWARE

Des Moines

A

Indianapolis

Cincinatti

WEST VIRGINIA

Washington DC

MARYLAND

MISSOURI

ILLINOIS

Louisville

VIRGINIA

St. Louis

KENTUCKY

NORTH CAROLINA

TENNESSEE

Nashville

ARKANSAS

Memphis

SOUTH CAROLINA

Little Rock

ALABAMA

Atlanta

MISSISSIPPI

Birmingham

GEORGIA

Jackson

LOUISIANA

Jacksonville

The hardiness-zone system illustrated here divides northern North America into ten zones based upon average minimum temperatures. The bands run generally in an east-west direction and range from the treeless area in the extreme north of Canada (Zone 1), where temperatures may fall to −50°F, to the southernmost tip of Florida (Zone 10), where minimum temperatures may be as high as 40°F.

New Orleans

FLORIDA

Gulf of Mexico

Miami

D0604465

| | Zone 1 below −50° | | Zone 3 −35° to −20° | | Zone 5 −10° to −5° | | Zone 7 5° to 10° | | Zone 9 20° to 30° |
| | Zone 2 −50° to −35° | | Zone 4 −20° to −10° | | Zone 6 −5° to 5° | | Zone 8 10° to 20° | | Zone 10 30° to 40° |

# WATERLILIES
## and other aquatic plants

# WATERLILIES
## and other aquatic plants

*Foreword by Frances Perry*

HENRY HOLT AND COMPANY
NEW YORK

To Nigel Davies
of Stapeley Water Gardens,
who died so tragically
in the summer of 1988

Text and photographs © 1989 by Stapeley Water Gardens
Foreword © 1989 by Frances Perry

Published in the United States by
Henry Holt and Company, Inc., 115 West 18th Street,
New York, New York 10011.

Originally published in Great Britain under the title
*Collins Guide to Waterlilies and other aquatic plants*.

Library of Congress Catalog Card Number: 89–45380

ISBN 0-8050-1170-6

Henry Holt books are available at special discounts
for bulk purchases for sales promotions, premiums,
fund-raising, or educational use. Special editions
or book excerpts can also be created to specification.

For details contact:

Special Sales Director
Henry Holt and Company, Inc.
115 West 18th Street
New York, New York 10011

First American Edition

Produced by the Justin Knowles Publishing Group
9 Colleton Crescent, Exeter, Devon EX2 4BY

Line illustrations: George Telford
Design: Michael Head

Printed in Portugal by Printer Portuguesa

1   3   5   7   9   10   8   6   4   2

# CONTENTS

# ACKNOWLEDGEMENTS

Grateful acknowledgement is given to all who contributed to the development of this book, particularly to Ray and Nigel Davies, the owners of Stapeley Water Gardens. Their staff, especially Peter Robinson and John Dutton, Steven Astbury, Ian Welch and Alwyn Mayor in the aquatic section, always gave without hesitation the benefits of their experience.

American members of the International Water Lily Society such as Perry Slocum, Peter Slocum, Charles Thomas, Pat Nutt, Paul Stetson, Barbara Dobbins and Don Bryne allowed the photography of varieties in their collections and gave first-hand knowledge of those varieties. Similarly, in the United Kingdom, Frances Perry, David Mason of Longstock Gardens and Norman Bennett always gave help and encouragement.

# FOREWORD

Everyone has an affinity with water which, it is generally conceded, is the source of life itself. Certainly we all use it for various purposes, water gardening being one of the more attractive examples.

However, water gardening is more than just gardening with water — more, much more! Water gardening is lily pads and submerged glades of ferny foliage, of dragonflies and dancing shadows on a mirrored surface. It is shafts of bright colour in the wake of darting fish, the music of a tumbling waterfall or a rippling stream, and above all, it is home for some of the world's most beautiful plants.

There are so many attractions. For one thing the water surface is constantly changing — dancing with staccato steps under the pounding of a rain shower, ruffled and dishevelled by strong winds, sombre-surfaced on dull days but sparkling like diamonds when the sun appears. There is music too in the hum of bees and chirruping of birds attracted to water, together with the louder notes emitted by fountains, and an undercurrent of rustling as the wind blows through waterside reeds. Then again, many different kinds of plants go to make a successful water garden, and it was these that first attracted and then exemplified for me its joys and fascination.

This was largely due to luck. In my student days, following a horticultural training it was obligatory to undergo a year's practical work before graduating. This had to be in an approved establishment, and I went to Perry's Hardy Plant Farm in Enfield, Middlesex, in the south of England. It so happened that Amos Perry — already well known for herbaceous perennials, rare bulbs and hardy ferns — was developing a department primarily concerned with water plants. Because of my interest he gave me overall charge of this expanding section, and soon I became highly involved with aquatics.

It was waterlilies that exerted the strongest appeal. One of the world's oldest and best represented plants — few countries lack a native species — they are beautiful to look at and variable as regards size, methods of propagation and times of flowering, with both day and night bloomers. Additionally, they have a long and fascinating history, which even the rose cannot surpass.

For early man waterlilies had two important properties. They supplied him with food and medicine, and, just as significant, they were of considerable importance — particularly in Asia and Africa — in his folklore, symbolism and religion. At times all peoples share similar hopes and aspirations. They yearn for immortality and they honour purity, and both qualities seemed to be apparent in waterlilies, which disappear from sight each year in the mud and slime of a dried-up river bed or pond, yet return pure and undefiled with the reappearance of rains and flood waters the following spring. For 5000 years, the Egyptian lotus (actually a blue waterlily or nymphaea, not the nelumbo of the Far East, which goes by the same common name) was venerated as a symbol of resurrection. This was because of its practice of folding the flower petals together at night and submerging the blooms beneath the water. The following day they reappear and open up as usual.

The well-filled seedpods of both types of lotus are believed to have inspired the cornucopia, ancient emblem of fertility, and such symbols as the Ionic capital, the Greek fret or meander and even the swastika have been attributed to waterlilies. Even today the tubers and seeds, both rich in starch and sugar, are used as food in some parts of the world, and it is interesting to reflect that the Biblical phrase 'Cast thy bread upon the waters, and thou shalt find it after many days' refers to the ancient practice of sowing nelumbo seeds in balls of clay before throwing them into the Nile to germinate. In due course, flour made from their seeds was turned into dough with some milk or water and baked as bread.

Although the Hanging Gardens of Babylon probably used water in some manner we cannot know this for certain. Certainly elaborate fountains and extensive water features have long been fashionable in parts of Europe, particularly in France and Austria, although these were normally constructed as spectacles rather than for the cultivation of aquatics. Early Britons seem to have shown only a gastronomic interest in stew ponds constructed to hold 'pikes and perches', although at the end of the Elizabethan era we find Francis Bacon complaining that although 'fountains are a great beauty and refreshment ... ponds mar all and make the garden unwholesome and full of flies and frogs'.

Three hundred years later William Robinson, so appreciated today by modern gardeners, went further. 'Unclean and ugly ponds deface our gardens,' he declared. 'Some have a mania for artificial water, the effect of water pleasing them so well that they bring it near their houses, where they cannot have any of its good effects. But they have instead the filth that gathers in stagnant water and its evil smell on many a lawn.' Even as recently as 1908, the eminent plant collector and gardener Reginald Farrer counselled readers as follows: 'Advice to those about to make a water garden – don't!'

What changed these views? Several things, such as a greater scientific understanding of how to obtain clean, clear water by balancing the plant and animal life, particularly in still pools. Better and cheaper methods of making pools have put water gardening within the reach of many more people, and the skills of a Frenchman called Joseph Bory Latour-Marliac, who, in the late 19th century, discovered the secret of producing new colours and types of hardy waterlilies, caused many people to put down pools in which to grow them.

Today, these factors have allowed water gardening to become a possibility for thousands. The pools can be little or large, formal or irregular in shape, with natural water features or fountains, streams and waterfalls that are quite artificial. The lightweight pond liners used to make pools watertight are easy to handle and readily fitted together. Another benefit of modern water gardening is the way in which water can be moved with the aid of pumps and electricity, so that waterfalls and fountains function efficiently and without waste, using the same water over and over again.

Today large lakes or small ponds, even a sawn-down wine- or beer-cask sunk into the ground is a potential water garden, but, unless it is appropriately planted, this is all it will be. According to its surroundings, various kinds of plants will be necessary – from the purely ornamental, deep-water aquatics like waterlilies and water hawthorns for open stretches of water to submerged oxygenators to maintain water clarity as well as act as nurseries for fish ova, and, later, sanctuaries to protect the fry from cannabilistic adults. Marginal aquatics will not only add to the effect and general interest but will mask those edgings where artificiality becomes apparent; floating plants cast shade, while bog plants link the pool with the rest of the garden proper.

Fortunately, most hardy aquatics are of easy culture and surprisingly free of pests or diseases, while – an added bonus – some waterlilies and the water hawthorns are deliciously fragrant, in some cases noticeable even before one reaches the poolside. However, all these elements demand a good knowledge of plants, the kinds to grow and the kinds to avoid. This is where a book on water plants by a reliable author is indispensable for all who garden with water – be it aquaria, still pool or stream garden.

*Frances Perry*

# INTRODUCTION

Aquatic plants, notably waterlilies (Nymphaeas) and lotus (Nelumbos), have played a major part in the stocking of gardens for many centuries. Water has long been a feature of gardens in Egypt, China, India and Japan, and it is not surprising that we find several historical references to the plants that grow in water.

Waterlilies, for instance, were known to have been grown in the temple gardens of Egypt, and the flowers were often used for decorating the tombs of the high priests some 1500–2000 years before Christ. Olive and willow leaves were found with waterlily flowers in the coffin of Tutankhamen, with papyrus forming the framework of a necklace of flowers. The hieroglyphics named lotus – not waterlily – and, as lotus is not indigenous to Egypt, the lotus referred to must have been either the blue tropical waterlily, *Nymphaea coerulea*, or the white-flowered *Nymphaea lotus*.

The gardens of Japan and China similarly made full use of waterlilies. The plants' intriguing habit of opening and closing their precious short-lived blooms between certain hours has always been a source of fascination. The fact that the blooms are frequently difficult to see except at close quarters and are often beautifully reflected in tranquil water may have contributed to their popularity in cultures known to have devoted long periods to solitary worship and meditation.

Nor did their value escape the herbalists. The thick fleshy root of the white waterlily contains tannin, starch, resin, gallic acid, tartaric acid, mucilage and ammonia; it is hardly surprising, therefore, that diligent herbalists harnessed such ingredients to a variety of uses. Frequent references are found to the waterlily's ability to calm the nervous and digestive systems, and Culpeper recorded that 'it settles the brain of frantic persons'. With additional alleged properties as an aphrodisiac, a few roots must have been a valuable standby to amorous young aquatic gardeners! There can be no disputing the use of waterlily roots as a dye – handle them frequently and you will soon know why!

Waterlilies are reputed to have influenced the patterns used on decorative friezes in ancient Greece, and the outline of the leaf was used extensively in *art nouveau* in the late 19th century. To this day waterlilies symbolize refreshment and tranquillity, as may be seen in the frequent advertising campaigns in which a white waterlily flower is linked to products associated with refreshment and relaxation.

The major step in the development of this beautiful flower occurred in the 19th century, when, after a century of indifference by garden writers, the discovery of a giant waterlily in South America heralded a new era in the popularity of, and interest in, waterlilies and other aquatic plants generally. Public attention was drawn to this giant waterlily when, in 1837, the leader of an expedition for the Royal Geographical Society, Sir Robert Schomburgk, sent back to Britain an account of this 'vegetable wonder' as he called it. It was 12 more years before viable seed were obtained and germinated at Kew, and it was flowered in Britain by Joseph Paxton, head gardener to the Duke of Devonshire at Chatsworth House in Derbyshire. Although this plant, which was named after Queen Victoria, is not a true waterlily, its cultivation in large greenhouses led in turn to a greater popularity of tropical waterlilies in heated conservatories. Joseph Paxton further encouraged this new plant fashion by developing a new red, night-blooming tropical variety, *Nymphaea* 'Devoniensis' (see page 97).

The breakthrough in the development of the hardy waterlily came in the 1880s when a Frenchman, Joseph Bory Latour-Marliac, began experimenting with the hardy varieties, crossing the European lily, *N. alba*, with the pink Cape Cod variety, *N. odorata* var. *rosea*, the yellow variety, *N. mexicana*, from Florida and the Swedish waterlily, *N. alba* var. *rubra*. Variety after variety of new vigour and colours were bred at his home in Temple-sur-Lot in southern France. Up to this time gardeners had had to be content with mainly white lilies, such as the native waterlily, *N. alba*, and a sweet-scented American species, *N. odorata*. Now there was colour in waterlilies, and, by the time Marliac died in 1911, he had created 70 new varieties of hardy waterlily. Sadly, all his records of years of patient selection, crossing and recrossing had been kept secret, but although those secrets died with him, he left beauty on a scale that it has not been possible to surpass.

With interest in waterlilies fast gaining momentum, the spotlight turned once more to the tropicals, and a new breeding programme was initiated at the Missouri Botanical Gardens in St Louis. Dr George Pring set about improving the tropical waterlilies as Marliac had done with the hardy varieties. The brief however was quite different: while the hardy lilies required more colour, the colours of the tropical lilies needed to be softened into more subtle shades. Much of the development continued in the U. S., with Civil War veteran W. B. Shaw transplanting wild waterlilies from his native Maine to his farm just outside the District of Columbia, and many more hardy hybrids were developed. With the help of his daughter Helen Fowler, who bred and painted waterlilies, some 10 more varieties were introduced. During the late 1880s the first waterlilies were offered in nursery catalogues when E. D. Sturtevant advertised Japanese tubers. Later, in 1895, William Tricker opened a nursery specializing in waterlilies near New York City.

The story of their development was by no means over, however. Following the pioneering successes of Marliac and Pring, other breeders on both sides of the Atlantic continued to refine and improve wherever possible. Beautiful seedlings emerged from nurseries and breeders, sometimes by chance, sometimes after long, patient hybridizing. The development has been made all the more worthwhile by the efforts and enthusiasm of the superb plantsmen and nurserymen who have inspired our great garden owners to be more adventurous and skilful in their planting and choice.

So what of the future of these beautiful plants? Perhaps a blue hardy waterlily, which has so far eluded the hybridists, will be bred. The International Water Lily Society is attempting to sort out some of the confusion in nomenclature and classification that has arisen over the years. As the Society recruits a greater international membership, the shared knowledge gained from symposia and newsletters should result in the appearance of more collections of labelled varieties to help reduce the all too common sight of unsuitable varieties choking the water's surface. Perhaps, too, there will be a revival of interest in the growing of tropical lilies in the small conservatories that are becoming increasingly popular. The waterlily has still a great part to play in the enhancement of our gardens, whether they are large or small.

# MAKING A WATER GARDEN

In contrast to the noise and movement associated with fountains and watercourses, there is a property of completely motionless water that instils a restfulness and peace to a garden. Water has an appeal in any setting, formal or informal, and, if enhanced by good design and planting, it gives an additional dimension to a successful garden that is hard to resist.

A great advantage of waterlilies and aquatic plants is their suitability for both formal and informal planting. In small gardens, where large areas of rectangular or square paving have been used, formally shaped pools will be more in keeping and easier to incorporate. The foliage of waterlilies contrasts beautifully with the striking vertical leaves of irises and other marginal aquatic plants used to soften the otherwise hard lines of paving. Long narrow pools are often the central feature in vistas of large gardens, and the long, clear stretches of water are often strengthened by the occasional grouping of leaves on the surface. But whatever the scale of your garden, do not compromise on the framework of the design. Keep the outline of the water in harmony with the setting and the planting will do the rest.

When water is used in a formal setting a fountain may be incorporated as a focal point. Waterlilies do not like too much turbulence on the water's surface and would certainly not thrive directly under the falling spray of a fountain. Only where the water area is large enough can one successfully

Groups of waterlilies enhance long, clear expanses of water

Waterlilies should not be sited where their leaves will lie directly under the spray
from a fountain

incorporate the two, and the overall design may well dictate where the
emphasis must lie – on moving water or on planting.

In small and shallow pools it is similarly not wise to compromise. If
fountains are the priority, it is often better to keep water clear chemically
than have green or murky water supporting poorly grown waterlilies.
There is, however, no escaping the fact that the long rectangular pool
provides one of the finest garden settings for waterlilies, and on a purely
practical note, the rectangular pool is one of the simplest shapes to
construct and surround with paving. Water's appeal in free informal
settings may be the reason why the kidney-shaped ponds, which epitomize
the water garden in so many small gardens, are so popular.

Although the kidney shape breaks away from the regular lines of formal design, these pools are frequently completely surrounded by crazy paving, which destroys the freedom to informal planting that the shape should bring to the garden. In a well-constructed informal pool there should be an easy transition from water to the moist or boggy soil surrounding it. It is in this marginal zone that the full potential of planting an informal water garden can be exploited. Although the formal pool can provide areas for such planting on shallow shelves within the water area, there is a special appeal in the planting at the water's edge. Such pools are ideal for plantsmen or plant collectors by providing a range of moisture levels for a wide variety of aquatic plants. Such an area is the perfect stage for irises, primulas, marsh marigolds, ornamental rushes and a host of beautiful lush marginal and moisture-loving plants. Such canopies of vegetation close to water also form ideal cover for a wide variety of wildlife in the garden.

The freedom an informal design offers in building irregular and complex shapes has to be treated with great care. Good design frequently stems from simplicity, and the design of pools illustrates this very well. When considering the shape of the pool, it is a good idea to use a rope or hosepipe to form the outline on the ground or lawn, so that you can examine the shape from different viewpoints. As one of the major attractions of water is in observing reflections, the shape and position of the pool in relation to the main viewing area is extremely important. This aspect is difficult to assess from a plan, and an old mirror on the proposed site could help to illustrate whether a desired feature will eventually be reflected by the water.

Keep the shape simple, and make it as wide as possible in the line of the main viewpoint so that you can see as much of the water surface as possible. A shape without too many curves is not only more attractive but is easier to construct, particularly if you are using a flexible liner.

### Siting the Pool

A problem confronting most owners of small gardens is to find the space to incorporate all their favourite plants. Allocating an area to a garden pool when room is limited may put water plants at a disadvantage when compared with the ease with which rose bushes or shrubs, for example, can be included. The list of site considerations that follows should not deter the prospective water gardener – they are not as forbidding as they may at first appear.

Consider the pool in relation to the window of a sitting-room or a room where you spend a lot of time. It is sensible to site a pool where it can be seen easily. Pools are relaxing to look at, particularly as they respond readily to changes of light and weather, and the reflections of waterlily blooms, sky and trees make careful siting well worth the time and effort. The birds and other wildlife that are attracted to the side of the pool make it a particularly desirable feature to be seen easily from the house.

There are, however, many other factors to take into account before siting the pool in what at first appears to be the ideal place.

First, a pool requires as much sunshine as possible if the planting is to flourish; this is particularly important for waterlilies, which can be very shy flowering in shady, cold sites.

Second, avoid a site directly under trees, where the problem is not only one of shade but of the deposits of leaves and small twigs, which fall into the pool and give off harmful methane gas as they decompose.

Third, if possible avoid what seems at first sight to be the natural place to site a pool – the lowest point of the garden. There is a likelihood of waterlogging in this position, and if a flexible liner has been used, it can be forced up into the water by pressure from the water table underneath. Moreover, if the pool is in the lowest part of a lawn, any fertilizers or weedkillers may drain into the pool and cause clouding or harmful toxicity.

Finally, it is an advantage if the site of the proposed pool is near to the electricity and water supplies and to a pathway for maintenance access.

## Size and Depth

Although the area of the pool is often limited by cost and the size of the garden, its long-term management is made easier as the volume and size increase. The smaller the water volume, the more difficult it is to achieve clear water through the correct balance of aquatic organisms. A small pool is more subject to rapid and frequent temperature fluctuations, which in turn stimulate the rapid growth of algae and subsequent greening. It is, therefore, recommended that the pool is as large as possible within the constraints of finance and design. Management aspects apart, a very small pool limits the choice of planting, and, unlike many other garden features, it is not easy to change the shape or size of a pool once it is installed. If possible, consider the minimum size to be something in the region of 40–50 sq ft (3.7–4.6 sq m), with a minimum depth of 18 in (46 cm). In pools that are larger than this, provided there is adequate depth, it is progressively easier to achieve the right biological balance in the water.

The depth of the pool should also be influenced by the need to ensure a stable water temperature and, therefore, the survival of plants and fish in the winter. The depth also affects the rate of growth of algae and consequent clouding, but there is no point in having a pool so deep that the

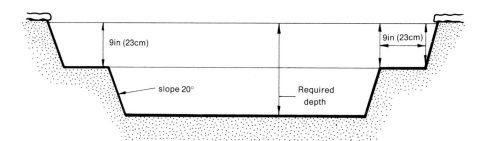

A pool profile. The minimum depth of a pool should be about 18in (46cm); even in very large pools it is rarely necessary to exceed a depth of 30in (76cm). Always ensure that the marginal shelves are horizontal

extra depth serves no function. As a guideline, assuming that the pool has been constructed with reasonably vertical side walls, the main area away from the marginal shelves needs to be approximately 18 in (46 cm) deep. Larger pools, over 100 sq ft (9 sq m), would justify a depth of 24 in (60 cm), and 30 in (76 cm) is the maximum depth required in even a small lake.

It is a misconception that a very deep pool is necessary for fish to survive and for waterlilies to flourish. The main requirement for fish in winter is not so much the depth of water but the availability of unpolluted water. To achieve this, ice must not be allowed to seal the surface for long periods and so prevent the natural escape of methane gas. Most waterlilies will grow in 18 in (46 cm) of water very successfully and will also benefit from the fact that the crowns are not so deep that they take a long time to warm up in the spring.

### Raised or Sunken Pools

Although it is natural to think of water below the level of the surrounding ground, certain formal designs lend themselves to raised pools. Such pools are ideally suited to formal patio areas, and they can either be free-standing or adjoin a wall where small waterfalls or spouting ornaments can be included. Such pools have the advantage of bringing the water surface and planting nearer to eye level, so that the beauty and scent of a waterlily may be more easily appreciated, especially by the elderly or disabled. There is also less risk of the very young enthusiast falling in a raised pool.

Because they are frequently constructed from brick sidewalls, raised pools provide the opportunity of sitting on the coping at the water's edge. However the limitations on size and depth already mentioned are particularly important here because of the greater risk of temperature variations above ground level.

### Constructing a Pool

It is not only improved varieties of waterlilies that have led to the current popularity of water gardening; a major factor has been the better construction materials available for small gardens. The new hard landscape materials produced from the technology of the 20th century and the availability of an improved range of plant materials have led to a revival of interest in aquatics on a scale not far removed from their use in the gardens of ancient Egypt.

Ponds and the cultivation of aquatics were once limited to low-lying land, where they depended on the depth of water available from the surrounding water table or on artificially compacted basins of clay. Waterlilies were occasionally seen in slow-moving rivers, but it was not until concrete was used to contain water that a significant change came in their popularity. Concrete had a great advantage over clay-puddled or mud-bottomed ponds for the growing of waterlilies: it provided some restriction to the hungry root system. A vigorous species or variety of waterlily will romp away in the rich soil base of an unlined pool, often creating an enormous quantity of leaf at the expense of flowers, as can be seen in innumerable large ponds and lakes where varieties like the common white waterlily form a tight mass of foliage that covers most of the water's surface.

In contrast, one of the finest illustrations of restrained waterlilies can be seen at Burnby Hall Gardens in Pocklington, Humberside. Here, two large lakes were lined with concrete, and the waterlilies were contained in brick planters three courses high on top of the concrete. Not only is this one of the finest selections of waterlilies in Great Britain, it also provides a most vivid example of balanced flowering in relation to growth. A large percentage of the water surface near the centre of the lakes remains clear, while the collection of waterlilies may be seen at closer quarters near the edge.

Although concrete is still used in pool making, it does have many disadvantages compared with the newer lining materials. Apart from the effort involved in mixing and laying concrete, its subsequent life expectancy is limited. Freshly made concrete pools should be coated with a sealant, and the water should be changed at least twice to ensure there is no toxicity to plants and fish. As the years go by, severe frosts take their toll of concrete pools, causing cracks at the water's surface. Repairs are time consuming and costly, and can be frustrating if a completely watertight seal has been difficult to achieve. Nevertheless, there are situations where concrete is successfully used, especially in modern formal designs within urban landscapes where concrete is already used extensively on site work.

One of the waterlily lakes at Pocklington, Humberside

*Pre-formed Pools*

The second type of waterproofing is the pre-formed rigid or semi-rigid pool of plastic or fibreglass, which is available in a variety of formal and informal shapes. These pools are the ultimate in ready-made kits, and they make possible the installation of a pond in very little time. The rigid fibreglass forms are strong, they are resistant to frost and ultraviolet damage, and they have a good life expectancy. Some of the semi-rigid plastic forms have been further improved recently and are now less susceptible to damage by cracking or splitting than fibreglass and carry 10-year guarantees.

All of these pre-formed pools can be very deceptive in size when displayed vertically in retail centres. Once installed in the garden, they appear very much smaller. Pre-formed pools have certain other limitations.

They are unlikely to be a first choice for the serious plantsman for whom the mass-produced shapes spoil some of the pleasure of creating an individual design. Although they are produced in several informal designs, they are better suited to the formal design edge, where paving rather than moisture-loving plants surrounds the water.

Nevertheless, the mass-production of pre-formed pools has brought the pleasure of water gardening to many home owners who may have been nervous about using a liner or concrete. Many small versions are bought on impulse, and, with good planting to blend them into their garden setting, they do offer an easy solution to aquatic growing.

*Flexible Liners*
The development of waterproof membranes or pool liners has given maximum flexibility in design and ease of construction. The three main types are made of polythene, synthetic rubber and plastic.

Polythene was the forerunner in the change from concrete pools to the use of flexible liners. Its main weakness was that it hardened and cracked when exposed to ultraviolet light. This weakened area inevitably occurred on the water line, where evaporation caused the water level to drop during the summer. The sun baked the polythene at this point, and it cracked and consequently leaked. Although the polythene liner could be covered with soil, sand or stone in an attempt to protect it from ultraviolet deterioration, this attention to detail was not always given, and in any case, the area just around the surface of the water proved a difficult and critical zone to protect. Polythene pools often became unsightly as ever-increasing bands of cracked polythene appeared at the water's edge, and the water level inevitably dropped with time.

Later, superior grades of PVC superseded polythene. These were much slower to break down under the influence of ultraviolet light, and they have been subsequently strengthened by laminating techniques and further reinforced with a fine nylon mesh between the laminated skins.

The ultimate development has been in the production of a rubberized sheet known as butyl. As there are various grades and some variation in manufacture, care must be taken to ensure that some of the cheaper products sold as butyl are free from ingredients that could be toxic to fish and weaker varieties of waterlily. For the average domestic pool, the minimum thickness should be 0.03 in (0.75 mm). Its matt black appearance makes it ideal for pond construction, giving the illusion of greater depth without garish colours. Butyl is manufactured in a sandstone colour, but in practice the standard matt black is the most popular as subsequent algae

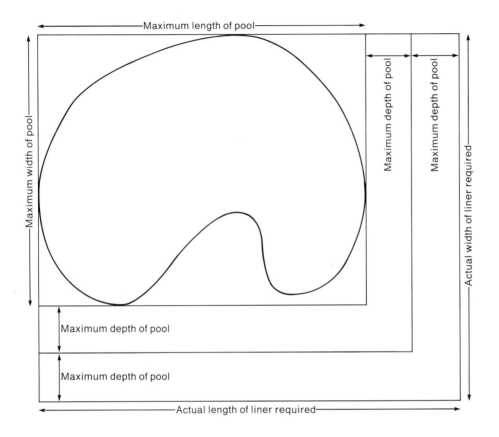

To measure the size of a liner, add twice the pool's depth to its length and width

growth covers the original colour with time. It is now used widely in commercial installations, particularly for lining reservoirs. Butyl is so superior to other materials used for liners that guarantees of its long effective life are often given.

One of its many advantages is its ability to stretch into the pre-formed shapes created in the excavation of the pool, thereby eliminating some of the folds created by cheaper liners. In addition, butyl does not deteriorate in ultraviolet light or frost, and it can be prefabricated into intricate shapes. If accidentally punctured with a garden fork it can be repaired in much the same way as a cycle tyre puncture. With a minimum life expectancy of 50 years, it is second to none as a material for pool construction.

To calculate the size of the liner required, add twice the pool's depth to the length and width of the pool required. For example, a pool whose overall dimensions are 10 ft by 7 ft (3.0 × 2.1 m) with a depth of 2 ft (0.6 m) will require a liner 14 ft by 11 ft (4.3 × 3.4 m). The pool can be any shape that will fit into a rectangle of 10 ft by 7 ft (3.0 × 2.1 m).

The length and breadth measurements are best checked by making the outline of the pool on the proposed site with rope, string or hosepipe. When you are satisfied with the shape and size, use sand or peat to mark the outline before the string or hose is removed.

For the plantsperson interested in a selection of marginal plants to grow in a bog area adjacent to the water, this is the time to consider its construction. If the size of the line is enlarged to the bog area required, the separation between the water and soil areas can be achieved by making a small retaining wall of rocks on top of the liner or by contouring the ground into a hump or shoulder before laying the liner. The bog area can then be filled with soil.

The opportunity to create this bog effect is one of the advantages of using a liner rather than a pre-formed pool in an informal area. Often one sees moisture-loving plants planted on the outside edge of a fibreglass or pre-formed pool where they have no more moisture than would be the case in any other part of the garden. One of the pleasures of informal water gardening lies in the association of several groups of plants, all with a varying degree of dependence on water. If this is taken into account at the design stage and an allowance made in the size of the liner for the bog plants, it can have a significant impact on the ultimate appearance of the water feature.

When you are satisfied with the site, size and shape of your proposed pool, begin cutting out just inside the line you have marked out: it is always easier to enlarge a hole than reduce it. Dig out the soil, making sure that the pool sides slope at a slight angle, which not only reduces the risk of the sides crumbling as you progress, but later helps the liner to settle on to the shape of the hole as the weight of water forces it down. An additional advantage of slightly sloped sides is that at times of severe frost the expansion of the surface ice is minimized as it tends to push up the slope, thereby reducing the possibility of damage at water level.

It is at this point that a shelf, some 9 in (23 cm) deep and approximately 9 in (23 cm) wide, should be excavated around the inside edge of the pool. This shelf provides the support for marginal plants in containers. After creating the shelf, continue the excavation, shaping the edges at a slight angle, until the desired depth is reached; this should normally be around 18 in (46 cm). If the topsoil is so fine that the sides fall away, some means of stabilizing the surface soil should be considered before further digging takes place. A thin skin of concrete is one method, and it can later be thickened to provide a stronger base if edging stones are used to surround the pool, or the walls could be more gradually sloped during excavation.

Check the proposed final water level regularly as you work, using a long, straight piece of wood to support a spirit level. Adjustments that may be necessary to the finished level are easier to make at this stage, before the liner is installed, by adding more soil to the lower areas or removing soil from the high parts.

Once the required depth and shape have been achieved, it is vital to check that the whole surface area is free from sharp stones or protruding sharp edges. If the ground is particularly weed infested, the entire area should be treated with a residual herbicide to prevent weed roots puncturing the liner. Once any offending objects have been removed, place a layer of soft sand or, better still, a covering of polyester matting, in the hole as a further cushion to protect the liner. The advantages of the underblanket of polyester matting lie in its relative cheapness and its longevity. Newspaper or other decomposable materials are sometimes recommended for this purpose, but for obvious reasons, they lose their effectiveness over time, rendering the liner at risk to pin-hole leaks some time after installation.

The liner is now ready to be inserted into the hole. Unfold it and, if you are working with plastic, drape it loosely over a paved area to absorb any warmth from the sun and so make it more pliable to work with. Butyl will stretch to shape without extra preparation. Then stretch the liner loosely over the pool, anchor it in place with stones around the edges and fill it with water. As the weight of the water on the butyl liner increases, the liner will stretch into the shape of the hole, thus helping to iron out the creases that inevitably occur with complex shapes. The stones anchoring the liner at the sides can be eased to allow the tension to be released and the weight of the water to be taken by the subsoil. An overlap of 6 in (15 cm) or more of the liner should now remain around the edge of the water level, and this can be tucked under surrounding soil or rocks or cemented under any flat edging stones.

In many pools, particularly formal pools, it is a good idea to support these paving edges at the water's edge with bricks or decorative walling stone. Cementing these supporting materials on top of the liner has the advantage not only of increasing the firmness of the edging stone, but also of disguising the liner at the water's edge. The unattractive, light 'tide mark', caused by the water level dropping with evaporation in the summer, will be less conspicuous on the stone surface than it would be on the black liner. The attention given to the detail of this edging, particularly ensuring that the finished water level is as near as possible to the bottom of the paving stones, will make a tremendous difference to the final result.

Formal pools benefit from the additional support of decorative bricks or paving stones at the water's edge

Two additional tips are worth mentioning at this stage. First, before cementing the edging stones into place, incorporate conduit or a length of waterproof electric cable under the paving for the later installation of accessories such as heaters or pumps. Second, if the pool is large, it is often easier to plant some of the deeper water plants such as oxygenators and waterlilies, which occupy positions near the pool centre, before completely filling the pool when handling and moving plants about become more difficult.

PLANTING THE POOL

The advice given for planting waterlilies and aquatic plants differs from that offered for plants growing in normal soils. Soil structure, soil acidity and fertilizer values should not be ignored, of course, but the creation of the correct biological balance of the surrounding large volume of water is as important as the properties of the soil surrounding the root system. Before exploiting this exciting opportunity to plant an exotic range of colourful plants into an aquatic environment, some time has to be spent in selecting and planting supporting submerged and floating plants that are of little ornamental value, but that are vital in their effect on the chemistry and appearance of the water.

This effect is best illustrated in natural pools, in which the clarity of the water seems to be linked to the abundance of submerged weed and small surface-floating plants like duckweed. This association of water clarity and ample water weed is the perfect illustration of the need to create similar conditions in artificial pools by planting both submerged weed and plants whose leaves lie on the surface of the water. The first priority is therefore to ensure from the outset that a high proportion of submerged and surface-leaved plants are planted and maintained. This is good news for the waterlily enthusiast, because the need for waterlily foliage in the successful water garden is justified not only on aesthetic grounds but also on scientific ones. No matter how imaginative and successful the marginal and waterside planting is, the effect of this planting can be completely spoilt by cloudy or dirty water; avoiding this is paramount.

The maintenance of water clarity is often described as having 'a well-balanced pool', and this is normally achieved by the reduction of microscopic, pool-inhabiting algae. The algae thrive in water where there is ample light and mineral salts on which to feed, and they are the most common cause of the 'pea green soupers' – those ubiquitous small green ponds that all too frequently appear in gardens. The results of insufficient preparation and inadequate planting, such ponds, often installed on impulse, are a common deterrent to a prospective water gardener, who associates water with midges, smell and pea green soup.

Contrast that impression with a well-stocked pool full of life and colour, the clear water reflecting nearby trees and the lush, fresh growth of marginal plants thrusting up at the water's edge. Few midge larvae survive where fish are introduced; any smell may be the subtle and elusive scent of waterlilies; and the crystal clear water allows glimpses of submerged and secretive life. But good water gardening requires care at the very earliest stage in the development of a new pool.

The early and rapid establishment of submerged and floating plants is

The reflections in the pool's surface of the sky and nearby plants are part of the charm of water gardens

crucial to the creation of a well-balanced pool, particularly if its construction coincides with a period of hot, sunny weather. The rapid greening of the water that can take place in these conditions often leads the new owner to drain and refill his pool in the erroneous belief that the clouding was the result of dirt. If possible, refrain from this draining. The clouding is almost impossible to prevent in pools created at the height of summer when the vital plant life has not yet had a chance to grow and become established.

Plant growth suppresses algae in two ways. First, the surface-leaved plants reduce the light on which algae depend. Second, by absorbing mineral salts themselves, the plants help to starve algae of their food. The plants also have other roles. In particular the submerged plants oxygenate the water, provide food and spawning areas for fish and support many forms of tiny beneficial organisms. Waste products from the fish are, in turn, absorbed by the plants and converted into plant proteins. This process, which is helpful to both fish and plants, helps to prevent the build up of toxic ammonia.

The reduction of surface light is therefore an important part of the planting strategy, although totally covering the water surface would do more harm than good by depriving plants and fish alike of sufficient surface light. Ideally, between half and two-thirds of the surface area should be covered by leaves either of surface-floating plants or of submerged plants with surface leaves such as waterlilies. This surface light filter is difficult to provide in a newly established pond, and in very small pools it may be necessary initially to introduce extra surface-floating plants. These can be netted off later as the pool becomes established.

The easiest method of establishing the two main types of plant – surface-leaved and oxygenating plants – may appear to be to provide a thick layer of soil on the bottom of the pond. Planting directly into this soil would seem to be both simple and relatively cheap. There is, in fact, a good case for using this technique in a wildlife pool of indigenous plants where a natural effect is intended. In the average ornamental pool, however, such a planting technique has the danger of later becoming unmanageable as the vigorous species spread rapidly and swamp the smaller plants. The subsequent removal of a plant becomes more difficult in this unconstrained system and results in the muddy disturbance of the pool bottom and the disentangling of mixed root systems.

It is therefore recommended that different species are planted into separate containers. The size of the container will vary according to the vigour of the plant. For vigorous waterlilies in large pools, for example, it is often necessary to construct containers *in situ*. Large rectangular, fibreglass tanks may be used for this purpose, provided there is sufficient manpower to lift them into the water if they have been planted beforehand. Most aquatic planting, however, is done in perforated plastic containers known as planting crates, which are capable of supporting all but the most vigorous species in their designated space. They are manufactured in a variety of sizes and have wide flat bases to help keep them stable under water. Ordinary plastic plant pots are not as successful for this purpose; the

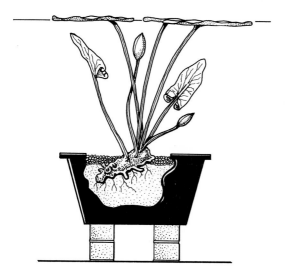

Planting a waterlily in a container

plants appear to prefer the mesh sides, which allow greater gaseous movement. Fine soil has a habit of dissipating through the sides of mesh planting crates, however. To prevent this it is sensible to use crate liners, which permit water and gases to percolate but contain soil movement. Hessian squares, which were for many years used as crate liners, are now being superseded by long-life synthetic materials with close weaving, which allows roots to penetrate the weave without damage. Many waterlilies flourish in containers that resemble large washing-up bowls, but plants are seldom sold in this way because of weight problems.

The compost used in the crates need be no more than good clean garden soil, which must be free of quick-acting fertilizers that encourage algae growth. If fertilizer is added, it should be of a slow-release type, releasing nutrients over a long period of time in small quantities. Rotted turf makes good aquatic compost, and it is the ideal medium for large containers holding vigorous waterlily roots. However, great care should be taken in checking the source of rotted turf in case a selective herbicide was applied before the turf was lifted; such a medium would cause residual damage to the lily and surrounding water. Specialist aquatic suppliers can provide a compost mix custom blended to suit aquatic plants. Standard composts sold for pot plant cultivation tend to have too much nutrient available, and they often have a large percentage of peat as a physical component. The nutrient increases the risk of algae growth as it leaches into the water, and peat and sand have no value to the roots of aquatic plants. It is essential to choose the planting material carefully, as changing compost in the crates is a difficult and smelly business if undertaken too often. If the soil is good enough in the first place, it should not need replacing for at least three years.

Although the technique for planting waterlilies and submerged oxygenating plants is different, the majority of plants growing in the shallower water at the edge of the pool, which are referred to as marginal plants, should be treated in much the same way as normal potted plants. The root system must be surrounded by sufficient soil in which to grow and leaves and aerial stems must be kept above the compost. Avoid covering the root system with too much or too little compost, but remember to firm as much compost into the container as possible.

This emphasis on firming the compost when planting into containers cannot be overstressed. First, because the compost is going to be waterlogged, it will shrink dramatically after being under water for some time. This shrinking is caused by the air in the compost being expelled under water and by the rapid breakdown of the organic content. It is possible to lift a container only days after planting and submerging it into the pool to find that it appears to be only half full of soil. The second reason for very firm potting into the containers is to ensure the plant is stable. During their relatively short season the rate of growth of aquatics is so fast that what started as a foot-high plant becomes three times that size within a few weeks. As the plants are surrounded by water, the stability enjoyed by plants in borders does not exist, and the taller plants soon blow over in windy conditions. In exposed sites the container itself has to be stabilized under water, but if the compost is loose within the container, the plants have no chance of remaining upright against wind. As mentioned earlier, as repotting should not be undertaken too often, every cubic centimetre of the container must be crammed with firm soil to keep the plant vigorous and healthy for as long as possible. After forcing all possible soil into the planting crate, cover the soil's surface with large stones or gravel to prevent the dry soil from floating away as the crate is lowered into the water and to provide some protection from inquisitive fish, which will disturb the soil.

Oxygenating plants are generally sold as bunches of weed, about 9 in (23 cm) long, with no root system but clamped together at the base with weighted material to prevent the bunches from floating to the surface. These bunches should be inserted and firmed into the soil in the planting crates to a depth of no more than 2 in (5 cm). The technique is similar to inserting cuttings into rooting compost in a propagator, when, instead of a trowel, a solid, tube-shaped piece of wood is pushed into the soil to make the planting hole. This handy tool is often referred to as a dibber, and the process of planting these unrooted stems is identical to the propagation process for softwood cuttings of other plants. Depending on the size of the crate, several bunches can be inserted. Normally, bunches of oxygenating plants can be inserted about 3 in (8 cm) apart in a crate, which should have a minimum depth of 4 in (10 cm). Each bunch generally contains several

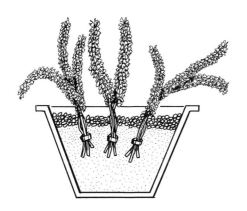

Oxygenating plants should be
inserted into planting
containers in bunches

unrooted stems, and, as a rough guide in a new pool, insert one bunch to every 2 sq ft (0.19 sq m) of water surface. They are normally inserted into the same type of soil as marginal plants, but as oxygenators can absorb food through their leaves from the surrounding water, they could be planted into an inert medium such as gravel, particularly if decent soil was difficult to obtain. If they are planted in soil, this should be covered with gravel as described for the marginal plants.

The planting of young waterlilies requires great care. They are frequently sold as pieces of root with a growing crown, and many plants are lost because the crowns are inserted too deeply into the planting soil and the containers too deeply submerged into the water. If bought as containerized plants, they are likely to be stronger and have leaves present on purchase. The whole plant should be transferred with as little disturbance as possible to a larger container. Plastic planting tubs specially made for waterlilies are available and they are ideal for the majority of varieties likely to be planted in small pools. They are approximately 14 in (36 cm) in diameter and $7\frac{1}{2}$ in (19 cm) deep.

To plant a waterlily, insert the root just under the surface of the soil but leave the crown or growing point exposed. The roots either grow sideways in the compost to form a thick, fleshy horizontal stem called a rhizome (more commonly seen in flag irises), or they form a thick, gnarled swollen cluster of buds, with the roots appearing below the buds rather than horizontally along a stem. These two forms of swollen root differentiate the types of hardy waterlily, but, for planting and growing purposes, as long as the crown is peeping out of the compost, it is not essential to distinguish between them. Once again firm planting must be stressed; loose planting could lead to the root later being seen floating on the surface. Good rich, fibrous topsoil should be used from pasture where there is no risk of the roots or seeds of pernicious aquatic weeds being introduced into the pool. If fertilizer is introduced into the planting compost, it should be of the slow-release type, supplying those plant foods that are associated with root development such as phosphorus. This is available as an organic fertilizer in the form of bonemeal, and a light dusting in the compost will help the new roots to become established more quickly.

Waterlilies are normally planted either at the bottom of the pool or, if it is a variety that only flourishes in shallow water, in a specially constructed container. Details of the optimum depth of water required for the various varieties appears in descriptions of the species and hybrid waterlilies (see pages 50–83). As the leaves of waterlilies are relatively short lived, they need not be retained on the newly planted plants; many of them will, in any case, be damaged, and they serve little purpose in the establishment of the young plants.

It is most important that the containers of freshly planted waterlilies are not immersed too deeply as the plants can be considerably weakened in their attempts to send new young leaves to the surface of the water. There are two methods of introducing the young plants into their new home. The first is to make a temporary plinth underneath the planting container to raise it in the water and thereby bring the growing point closer to the surface. Two or three courses of brick base make a good temporary support.

Support newly planted waterlilies and other plants on bricks until they are established

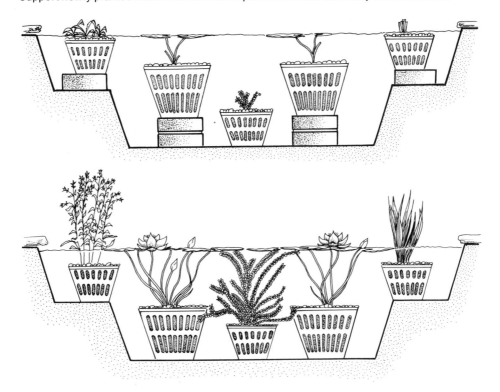

After a few weeks, when several lily pads are on the surface, the temporary support can be removed gradually, one course at a time, until the planting container rests directly on the pool bottom. The second system requires the water level of the pool to be lowered as the containers are placed on the bottom of the pond in their permanent quarters. As the waterlilies grow, the water level can be increased until it reaches the required level and the lily has made sufficient growth.

If either of these two systems proves to be impracticable – as might happen when new varieties are being introduced into a large established pool or lake where temporary supports cannot be made under water – wear waist-high waterproof waders and carry established plants in large containers to the desired position and lower them to the bottom of the pool.

Generally, aquatics should be planted between April and September. When this coincides with a period of hot sunny weather, ensure that any submerged plants are not out of the water for longer than is absolutely necessary, as severe shrivelling occurs if they are exposed to sunshine and air. If plants ordered by post arrive at an inconvenient time and some delay is likely before they can be planted, insert them into buckets or containers of water as a temporary measure rather than leaving them in the plastic bags, where sweating and rotting may occur. There are no hard and fast rules governing the density with which waterlilies should be planted as their cover of the surface water relates to the vigour of the variety. It is a matter of personal preference whether there is one vigorous variety or two or three dwarf varieties or those of medium vigour. The most important consideration is not to overplant with too many or with too vigorous varieties. All the best examples of good waterlily planting allow plenty of room between varieties and for equal areas of clear surface water to frame them.

Similarly there are no hard and fast rules regulating the quantity of marginal plants to use. Many species are fast growing, however, and allowance should be made for this when spacing them to do justice to their aesthetic value.

As already mentioned, oxygenating plants do have more precise requirements. One bunch should be planted for every 2 sq ft (0.19 sq m) of surface area, but provided they are all planted in containers, it would certainly do no harm to exceed this figure to ensure a more rapid build up of oxygen levels in the water, which is particularly important if fish are to be introduced quickly. Too many oxygenators would, by the end of a summer, become out of hand and the decomposition of their foliage in the winter could lead to maintenance problems and excess methane levels in the water.

It is a simple matter to remove some containers in the late autumn if excess growth has occurred. Oxygenators should not be planted deeper than 3–4 ft (1 m), and they thrive between 18 and 24 in (46–61 cm).

It is highly desirable to mix the species, as some species like the starwort (*Callitriche autumnalis*) continue oxygenating throughout the winter, and hornwort (*Ceratophyllum demersum*) is less susceptible to fish nibbling the young growth. These two species should be included in any collection of oxygenators if fish are already present. Many submerged plants act as oxygenators, but only about half a dozen are normally sold specifically for the purpose. Although mentioned in a later chapter, the oxygenators to include in a mixture for a new pond are: *Ceratophyllum demersum* (hornwort), *Eleocharis acicularis* (hairgrass), *Elodea canadensis* (Canadian pondweed), *Fontinalis antipyretica* (willow moss), *Lagarosiphon major*, *Myriophyllum verticillatum* (milfoil) and *Ranunculus aquatilis* (water crowfoot).

## Waterlilies

The flowering aquatic plants collectively known as waterlilies were among the first splashes of colour that man noticed on this earth. Although earlier plant forms were in profusion, the process of evolution seems to have favoured waterlilies, which quickly developed to their present form.

Waterlilies bear the generic name of Nymphaea, which, according to Greek legend, is derived from *nymphaia*, a flower that arose from a nymph who had died of jealousy. In the first century A. D. the Roman historian and naturalist, Pliny, associates waterlilies with a nymph who had died from unrequited love for Hercules.

The waterlily family – Nymphaeaceae – is a very old plant family of water or marsh plants, which are scattered widely around the world. The family contains many strikingly beautiful flowers and interesting plants, of which four other genera – Euryale (gorgon plant), Nelumbo (lotus), Nuphar (brandybottle lily) and Victoria (giant Amazonian waterlily) – will be described later in this book.

There are at least 40 species of waterlilies distributed throughout almost the whole world including the tropics. Most, especially the hybrids, have brightly coloured flowers, and as a rule it may be said that the more colourful the flower, the more complex its genetic history. Flowers vary in size, but they are always in proportion to the size of leaf, ranging from 1 in (2 cm) in diameter in the pygmy varieties to 12 in (30 cm) in some of the tropical varieties.

Waterlilies are split into two main groups, the hardies and the tropicals,

'Norma Gedye', a hardy waterlily that blooms consistently over a longer period than many other hardy varieties

the main difference being in the temperature requirements for each type. Tropicals are at risk below temperatures of 70° F (21°C). Hardy lilies can be planted outside in temperate zones from as early as April without fear of damage by frost. Many of the varieties of hardy waterlily can tolerate quite deep, cool water, particularly the common white waterlily, *Nymphaea alba*. Tropical lilies, on the other hand, must be planted in late spring in warm shallow water. Once started, they quickly catch up on their hardier cousins and continue to flower late into the autumn, even into early winter if they are indoors or in a warm sheltered spot.

Many waterlilies, particularly the tropical flowers, are scented. The scent of the hardy species *Nymphaea odorata* has been likened to violets, tea roses or lily of the valley, while the scent of *Nymphaea tetragona* has been likened to the smell of tea.

The hardy waterlilies form vertical or horizontal creeping rootstocks, which are mainly uniform in thickness in the horizontal forms (as in the odorata and tuberosa species) or club-like in the vertical forms (as in the Marliac hybrids). These rootstocks, called rhizomes, can grow to be as thick as a man's arm. They grow horizontally and are banana-shaped with patterns on the surface caused by scars made by fallen leaf stalks.

The tropical species and varieties form a different type of rootstock. It takes the form of an oval tuber, ranging in size from a small walnut to a large egg. If growth dies down in cooler water in the winter, these tubers can be stored like those of a dahlia, in moist sand in a warm place until late spring.

The long, supple leaf stalks that arise from the rootstocks support round, oval or heart-shaped leaves, often referred to as pads, which float on the surface of the water. The leaf stalks are capable of growing quickly in response to an increase in the depth of the water. The horizontal floating leaves or pads can vary in size and shape according to age. They are leathery in texture, and, although easily torn, are capable of surviving heavy storms. The leaf margins also vary, some varieties having wavy or toothed edges, while others have edges that curl slightly. All of the floating leaves are generally short lived, being replaced regularly throughout the growing season. The upper surfaces are mainly green and covered with a waxy, waterproof layer. Within this layer are the breathing pores of the leaf, which are known as stomata. Many of the hybrid varieties have variegated leaves, some of which, like the marbled leaves of a rare variety called 'Arc-en-ciel', are so spectacular that they are grown for their foliage alone. The undersides of the leaves, which have an almost magnetic attraction to the water's surface, are bluish green, often almost reddened by anthocyanic colouring substances. Such substances, which are also found in many variegated plants and blue flowers, increase the efficiency of the leaf by trapping for photosynthesis sunlight that would otherwise filter through to the water underneath.

'Arc-en-ciel', a rare variety, grown more for its foliage than its flowers

The beautiful flowers either float on the surface as in the case of the hardy species and varieties or are held above the surface as in the tropical forms. When the plant has become overgrown, flowers that should normally be surface floating may rise above the water on their stems. Each flower consists of a large number of spirally arranged flower parts, which radiate from the centre. First are numerous and often highly coloured stamens; these are surrounded by petals, which in turn are surrounded by an outer ring of thicker petals referred to as sepals. The colourful petals surround the equally attractive stamens or male reproductive organs, which bear the pollen. These petals and stamens are supported by the structure known as the receptacle, which somewhat resembles a hollow cone. Within this receptacle are the female reproductive organs, collectively known as carpels. Like the petals and stamens, they are also arranged in circles, but they are embedded in the flesh of the receptacle, giving the appearance of a single fruit.

The flowers are self- or cross-pollinated, and the fertilized carpels ripen under water until mature, when they break up and are dispersed as seeds.

There are a wide range of flower colours with many variations in pastel shades, although blue, green and purple flowers have not yet been developed in the hardy varieties. The hardy forms open their flowers during the day, close them at night, then reopen them on the second, third and sometimes fourth days. The position of the stamens gives a clue to how old the flower is. On the first day the stamens are erect, in some cases even pointing slightly away from the centre of the flower. As each day passes, the stamens slowly bend or collapse towards the centre, until they totally cover the receptacle at the end of the flower's lifespan. On warm sunny days during late summer, it is often difficult to find a flower free of the insects that have been lured to the rich nectar that is present in the flower's receptacle.

Some varieties have bicoloured flowers; others have the added charm of flowers that change colour with time, making the identification of varieties a difficult process for all but the expert.

A good example of a 'changeable' variety is the medium-flowered, Marliac type, 'Comanche', which starts out a rich rose-apricot colour, becomes darker and more vivid and finally turns a glowing coppery bronze, having, as one admirer observed, 'a heart of fire'. Flower colour also varies quite dramatically as the plant becomes more established and vigorous. This characteristic often leads to initial disappointment in the performance of a young waterlily variety, when the colour does not match up to the picture in the catalogue or flowers of the same variety in an established and well-fed situation. With time, however, the colours will attain their full beauty, particularly if the plant gets plenty of sunshine during the first two summers.

The value of a sunny position for all waterlilies cannot be overstressed. Flowering capacity drops markedly in shaded sites; sunshine should strike the pool for at least half of the day, so shade-creating trees and shrubs should always be sited on the north side of a lily pool. Two varieties sometimes recommended as more shade tolerant than most are 'Comanche', a variety with medium, deep orange blooms, and the popular yellow variety *N. marliacea* 'Chromatella'. Although each flower lasts for only a few days when fully open, like the leaves, they are constantly being replaced during the growing season.

The tropical waterlilies are the flamboyant cousins of hardy forms. They could be considered as bigger, brighter and better in most respects, having beautifully coloured and veined leaves with edges that are frequently crimped, fluted or frilled.

The elusive blue of the hardy waterlilies is present among the broad range of colours displayed by the tropicals, and even purple is represented. The tropicals produce many times more flowers per plant than the hardy forms, and they hold their superb flowers above the water surface on tall, strong stems.

There are two forms of tropical waterlily – the day-flowering and night-flowering varieties. The fragrant, day-flowering forms normally open before mid-day and close about dusk. The night-blooming varieties complete the full cycle of flower over 24 hours by flowering at completely the opposite times, from dusk to noon the following day. The night-blooming varieties have a magical quality when seen subtly illuminated on warm summer evenings. The famous American garden at Longwood in Pennsylvania masters this technique superbly. The conservatories and gardens are open well into the dark evenings when they take on a new character. Longwood has an excellent collection of waterlilies, but the night-blooming varieties, in association with the other aquatics in the floodlit gardens, are a sight to be remembered. There can be few more romantic sights than the huge white flowers of the giant tropical waterlily, Victoria, and night-blooming waterlilies by moonlight.

It can be seen that by combining the three groups of waterlily mentioned it is possible to have a succession of flowers from early spring to autumn, provided there is some form of heated glass protection. Under favourable conditions, some varieties of tropical waterlily will flower all year round. There has recently been a marked renewal of interest in conservatories, and this could signal the revival of interest in the tropical waterlilies once associated with the 19th century.

The hardy, white, fragrant *odorata* forms could start the spring display, and they would be followed by the many shades of later blooming hardies. The day-blooming tropicals could start the indoor display in early summer, to be joined in mid-summer by the night blooming types. Where there is poor light in a conservatory, the day-blooming tropical varieties 'Director George T. Moore', a deep purple flower, and 'Isabelle Pring', a beautiful globular white flower, are reasonably shade tolerant. Several varieties seem to thrive better under glass, a good example being the blue-flowered *N. daubenyana* (often also called 'Dauben' or 'Daubeniana'). It is not uncommon to see six or eight flowers on one plant at the same time, and provided the water temperature is kept above 70°F (21°C), this plant will remain flowering almost continuously for many years.

Every few years, all forms of waterlily will benefit from the removal of old, inefficient roots and the replanting of the young growths into fresh compost. Older plants frequently crowd pools, and the clustered masses of leaves, which can be seen thrusting out of the water, signal the need for division.

At the same time flowering decreases. The flowers become smaller and less vivid, and the leaves too become smaller and lose their deep green lustre. Once lifted, the old growths can be cut off and the new healthy young growth planted into fresh compost. If several young plants are required instead of simple replacement, the young side shoots or buds (eyes) can be cut off and planted into smaller containers. Seed is seldom used as a method of propagation. Only very few species set seed successfully and the hybrid varieties are almost completely sterile. The dwarf *N. pygmaea* is one of the exceptions, but the masses of seedlings produced can only be justified when there is a need for a very large number of offspring.

Although the tropical waterlilies set seed more easily than the hardy forms, propagation is more often practised vegetatively by removing the small tubers that form at the base of the crown. These small tubers are the plant's normal method of overwintering, and, as mentioned earlier, these tubers can be stored in moist sand before being planted in the spring in a heated aquarium in small pots with the water level just covering the pots. Once growth gets underway, the young plants can be transferred to larger planting bowls in slightly deeper water until conditions are warm enough and the plants strong enough for them to survive in their deeper and more permanent quarters.

A viviparous leaf

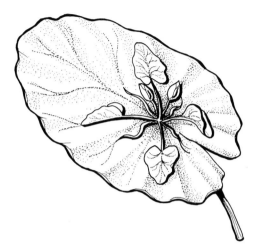

An interesting method of self-perpetuation exhibited by certain tropical varieties occurs when some of the leaves produce on the leaf surface small plantlets, which grow from the central leaf vein. The system closely resembles the technique of the piggy-back plant, *Tolmeia menziesii*. Flowers may be produced while the plantlet is still attached to the plant, making an interesting picture of parent and children flowering simultaneously. Varieties capable of this phenomenon are described as having viviparous leaves, and certain varieties, like *N. daubenyana*, are notably more prolific than others in their production of these young plantlets. Full advantage can be taken of the habit as a form of propagation; remove the leaves and pin them to the surface of a small potful of compost. The top of the pot should be kept just below the water's surface to enable the plantlet to form young aquatic roots into the compost without being drowned. An alternative method is to position the pot of compost under the leaf while it is still attached to the parent plant. Once rooting into the compost has occurred, the leaf stalk can be cut and the offspring removed by the technique that is used for strawberry runners.

Both types of waterlily require ample feeding throughout the summer months and care to ensure that they do not succumb to pests and diseases (see pages 44–9). Feeding by means of concentrated fertilizers is more difficult than with terrestrial plants, as the dissolving of the nutrient salts into the water frequently results in clouding. This is caused by the rapid build up of algae, which thrive on dissolved salts, and the presence of too many algae is not only unsightly, but can be harmful as certain filamentous algae can reduce the vigour of the waterlily. In the first summer after planting it is unlikely that the young plant will have exhausted the food value of the compost if it was planted in a sufficiently large container. If, however, a small crate was used for a vigorous variety, feeding may be necessary quite soon after planting. Proprietary concentrated fertilizers specially made for waterlilies are available. These should be pushed into the soil of the planting crate to a minimum depth of 6 in (15 cm). Their efficacy is based on the slow release of the correct plant foods.

Correct feeding demands that the health and growth of the plant are assessed before the form of nutrition is determined. If the lily is making ample, lush growth and produces deep green leaves frequently, it is unlikely to need more nitrogenous feeding, which would encourage even more growth at the possible expense of flowers. This is particularly true of waterlilies that are rooting freely into the mud at the bottom of the pool. If such a pool is further enriched by the silt or sediment from a river inlet, the food value in the sediment is likely to be high, and any feeding should relate to flower production rather than to growth.

Bonemeal is frequently recommended as a fertilizer for waterlilies because it is relatively slow to release its nutrients and it encourages the plant to develop a strong root system. Concentrated fertilizer is best applied by mixing pinches with soil or clay and water into sticky, golfball-sized lumps, which, when dry, can be inserted into the compost in much the same way as the proprietary kinds. There are, however, more readily available proprietary fertilizers that are sold for adding to composts and soils where plants and trees require small amounts of food over long periods. As these products also have trace and minor elements included, they can be useful for feeding older waterlily plants. Many of these fertilizers are pelleted, and the nutrient dissolves slowly out of layers of the pellet. Only small quantities are required, no more than 1 oz (28 gm) for a planting crate.

Avoid fast-acting nitrogenous fertilizers. These not only release their available nitrogen too quickly and promote excessive algae growth, but also have a tendency to make the water more acid. Ideally, waterlilies like slightly alkaline water, which falls between the extremes of acidity and alkalinity in which algae flourish.

As waterlilies dislike turbulence of any form, protect the plants from wind wherever possible and avoid planting near waterfalls or fountains. If they are grown in a very slow-moving current, plant rushes and other similar vegetation upstream of the lily to stem the flow around the leaves.

During the growing season the plants look much better if the pads that are dying back are removed regularly. Cut the leaf stalks as low as possible under the water. Never pull away the leaf stalks as this could tear tissue, particularly near the rootstock, and cause fungal infection. Apart from improving the appearance of the pool, the regular removal of vegetation

The principle of ensuring the correct balance of oxygenating and surface plants applies to small pools just as it does to large ones. Dwarf and pygmy varieties of waterlilies are ideal for pools in tubs or barrels

that will decay under the surface is advantageous, especially before the winter, because the accumulation and rotting of such tissue produces methane in the water. Old flowers, therefore, should similarly be removed whenever possible.

The dwarf or pygmy varieties are excellent subjects for growing in tubs or barrels and bring the scope of a miniature water garden within the boundaries of a balcony or small yard. Provided there is sufficient sunshine and the correct variety is chosen, there are few other constraints on the success of such a venture. Maintain the same principles as in the construction of a larger pool – provide some oxygenators and a marginal plant to give some height; ensure there is no residual toxicity in the barrel's construction; and maintain an adequate depth of water – and the whole feature will become a self-supporting aquatic world.

PESTS AND DISEASES OF
WATERLILIES

The chemical control of pests and diseases afflicting waterlilies is made more difficult by the susceptibility of the other occupants of the water, particularly fish. If pest damage reaches serious proportions, the handpicking of infected areas is recommended. Fortunately, waterlilies are not prone to a wide range of pests and diseases causing serious damage, and when they are present, the fish themselves control many of the insect pests by devouring the larvae. Many successful and well-established water gardens have never had a chemical spray near them for years, as the vigour of the plant and the balanced ecological environment in which they live provide a natural resistance to pest and disease. As with most plants, if feeding patterns and the conditions of growth are as natural as possible, the level of infection or damage will not get out of hand. In extreme cases, where chemical measures of control have to be resorted to, try to remove the plants from the water first, and treat them by immersing in a bucket of dilute pesticide or fungicide. After being immersed for a few hours, thoroughly rinse the whole plant before returning it to the pool. While the plants are out of the water, don't waste the opportunity to remove any damaged or badly diseased tissue or leaves, particularly if waterlily crown rot (see below) is suspected.

**Pests**

*Waterlily aphids (Rhopalosiphum nymphaeae)*
Although several aphids or greenfly attack waterplants, this small black species can be particularly troublesome. It is not only disfiguring but also smothers the leaves in large colonies. As aphids suck sap to feed, a heavy infestation inevitably reduces the efficiency of the leaf and results in a loss of vigour. In common with many other forms of aphids, the overwintering eggs are laid on trees; in this case, plums and cherries are the hosts. In the spring the eggs hatch into winged females, which fly to water and give birth asexually to further generations of wingless offspring. The colder autumn days signal a change, and winged forms are born. The cycle is completed when eggs are laid away from the lily on the nearby trees. Winter spraying with ovicides (egg-killing sprays) of nearby dormant members of the Prunus (plum) family helps, as does the physical removal of the early colonies from the leaves in the spring.

If no livestock is present in the pool, contact washes of pyrethrum-based insecticides or nicotine soap should be given early in the season if there is any infestation. Alternatively, a light spray on the waterlily foliage with a dilute proprietary oil solution will smother the pests but not harm fish or other inhabitants of the pool. If fish are present, carefully read the instructions of any proposed spray. Spraying the leaves forcibly with a fine jet of fresh water dislodges vast quantities of aphids, which are readily devoured by any fish present.

*Waterlily beetle (Galerucella nymphaeae)*
These beetles are by no means as widespread as aphids, but once a colony is established on a collection of lilies it becomes increasingly difficult to eradicate. Small dark brown beetles, about twice the size of a ladybird, overwinter on poolside vegetation and visit the waterlilies in June. Eggs are laid in groups on the leaf surface, and after a week or so small, dark brown larvae, which resemble small slugs, emerge and feed voraciously on the foliage. The surface layers of cells on the foliage are stripped by the larvae, and this causes rapid rotting of, and gives a tatty appearance to, the leaves. Several generations occur in one season, and the aerial foliage of surrounding aquatic vegetation provides the ideal home for the larvae to pupate. Again, jetting the foliage forcibly with fresh water in summer dislodges the larvae, which have little chance of survival in the water if fish like golden orfe are present. In addition, cutting back surrounding marginal vegetation in the winter reduces the overwintering hosts. An alternative method is to spray all waterlilies in the infested pool with a solution containing powdered *Bacillus thuringiensis* bacteria (available through specialist aquatic suppliers), which parasitize the larval caterpillars and kill them. The bacteria are completely non-toxic and harm only the larvae.

*Brown china mark moth (Nymphula nymphaeata)*
The symptoms of the mark moth damage are holes in the foliage, particularly around the leaf margins. The holes are caused by the larvae of the insignificant and small brown adult moth, which has a 1 in (2 cm) spread of orange-brown wings patterned with white. It lays clusters of eggs close to the edge of the leaves, and the eggs soon hatch into small white larvae. The insect does most damage in the larval stage, when it bites off pieces of leaf to make a protective case for the silk cocoon it occupies in a small, floating home. From such a home, it can drift around the edges of the waterlily leaves and have the odd meal from the edges of the foliage until it pupates. Eggs are laid on the undersides of the leaves, and the new breed of caterpillars feed there until they, too, make cases out of pieces of the lily foliage for their cocoons.

The closely related china mark moth (*Nymphula stagnata*) also damages the plant when the small caterpillars eat into the leaf stems. The damage done by both species is normally not too serious, particularly if fish are present. Control is by the removal or netting of the floating homes if seen, and, if damage is very severe, the removal of all the adult leaves. This temporary defoliation enables the young leaves to grow away with less risk of infection; or use *B. thuringiensis* as above.

### Leaf mining midge (Cricotopus ornatus)
A severely disfiguring pest, the leaf mining midge lays eggs on the surface of the leaves. The tiny, slender and almost transparent larvae then proceed to tunnel in a random fashion in the surface tissue. If the infestation is heavy, the leaves can be completely skeletonized, which could be serious on young plants of the pygmy varieties. Leathery, thick-leaved varieties seem more resistant to attack. Control is by removing damaged leaves as soon as the tunnelling marks are noticed. If this does not check the infection, use *B. thuringiensis* as above or remove the plant and dunk it into a dilute insecticide, rinsing it thoroughly before returning it to the pool.

### Caddis flies (Trichoptera)
A pest that is a nuisance only to the waterlily grower who excludes fish from the pool, caddis fly larvae consume just about everything growing in the water. The larvae, however, are aquatic and a favourite food of fish, particularly goldfish, which prevent the larvae from reaching any significant numbers. The adult flies resemble brownish moths, but differ from moths in having a sparse covering of small hairs on the wings instead of scales. There are nearly 200 species of caddis fly, which are mostly nocturnal and range in size from $\frac{1}{4}-\frac{1}{2}$ in (6–12 mm). The flies lay their eggs during the evening, embedding them in long cylindrical tubes of protective jelly on submerged or aerial foliage, sometimes with parts of the tube dangling in the water. When the larvae hatch from the eggs, they spin a web of silk around themselves and disguise or protect these shelters with pieces of broken plant, old snail shells or specks of sand and gravel. As it gets bigger, the larva keeps adding to its case and never fully emerges from it. *B. thuringiensis*, used as described above, is a good control.

### Snails
It seems at first sight confusing to include snails as pests when they are frequently to be seen for sale alongside aquatic plants. They are sold because of their scavenging role in a pool, where they help to clean up algae, decaying plant material, surplus fish food and dead or drowned animal matter such as worms and fish. There are, however, many schools of

thought on their overall value and the policy of deliberately introducing them into a pond.

There seems little doubt that one species of snail, the ramshorn (*Planorbis corneus*), is safe to introduce and will perform the true scavenging role without causing any damage to waterlilies and other aquatic vegetation. As its name suggests, the shell resembles the circular horn associated with a type of sheep, although a flattened catherine wheel is the best description I have seen used. The shell is carried vertically as the snail meanders around the pool, cleaning up the algae like a little vacuum cleaner. The black Japanese snail, *Viviparis malleatus*, is another excellent pool scavenger that will clean away decay but spare aquatic plants.

Other snails, however, may not confine their diet to algae. Although the common pond snail or freshwater whelk (*Limnaea stagnalis*) is a very efficient and busy scavenger, it can become a pest if there is insufficient alternative food and it turns its attention to young waterlily leaves and the foliage of submerged oxygenating plants. It can be identified by its pointed shell, rather like a spiral dunce's hat, on which the spiralling is in the opposite direction to nearly all the other snail shells. It is only small, no larger than the tip of a little finger, which makes it efficient in reaching between foliage in search of algae that other larger snails find difficult to reach. The pointed shell is only 1–2 in (2–5 cm) high, but it protects the potential delicacy from large fish. Like the ramshorn, it sticks its eggs on the undersides of waterlily leaves in long strings of jelly, from which the young snails emerge in three or four weeks. The ramshorn's egg jelly tends to be in flat pads, while the common snail jelly is in longer strands. In a new, small ornamental pool, where plants are just establishing themselves, it would be unwise to introduce the common snail; the chances of their natural introduction are high anyway. In large pools, lakes or wildlife pools with masses of vegetation there is less problem. If they do become a problem, float cabbage or lettuce leaves on the surface of the water for 24 hours. The snail population will be attracted to the bait, which can be easily removed together with the snails.

*Mosquito larvae*

Although much rarer now, mosquito larvae can be a problem for young plants as they appear in early summer when they attack the leaves and buds. Unless the larvae are checked, the leaves will turn yellow and the buds will fail to mature. Again, if fish are present there should be no problem; introduce golden carp, golden rudd, golden orfe or even our native minnow.

## Diseases
### Leaf spots
Several fungi attack waterlily leaves and, if allowed to develop unchecked in warm wet weather, they can cause the pads to die. All types start as dark patches on the leaves, one form causing the margins of the leaves to dry and turn up. In the early stages of attack spray a mild solution of Bordeaux mixture on the pads every other day for a week. If spraying is not possible, remove the infected leaves quickly and burn them.

### Waterlily crown rot
A serious fungus disease, particularly to a grower of waterlily collections, waterlily crown rot is a species of Phytopthora, a disabling and widespread disease. In the case of the waterlily, the fungus causes the crown and stem base to blacken and rot. It spreads like wildfire through a collection, and, as the infection is below water level, a wary eye must be kept for loss of vigour and early yellowing of the foliage. Further examination of the crown and stems will reveal rotting black, jelly-like tissue and a vile, unmistakable smell, even when roots appear healthy. Routine dipping in fungicides for prevention is practised in commercial nurseries, but in the small pond the only remedy is to remove and burn the infected plant and to replace it and its soil. Seek professional aid for collections suffering from crown rot. A Japanese system of growing waterlilies involves growing the plants on a ridge and furrow system, similar to potatoes in fields, during which they are repeatedly flooded and drained. Imported rootstocks from this system initially show good vigour, but later they are more susceptible to the crown rot when submerged. The most susceptible varieties are 'Laydekeri Fulgens' 'Marliacea Ignea', 'Ellisiana' and 'Rose Arey'.

## Water discoloration
Although not fungal infections, the following three conditions affect the pleasure that can be gained from a waterlily pool: green water, dark or milky water and blanket weed. If the water turns green, check that the surface and submerged planting adequately deprives the offending algae of mineral salts. As a temporary measure, algicides may be used, but the water will probably turn green again in time if the planting balance is incorrect. To control dark or milky water remove rotting vegetation from the base of the pool. If there is so much weed that it blankets the pool's surface, remove with a net or twirling on a forked stick or rake. Algicides have been specifically developed to control blanket weed, but some products damage dwarf and weak-growing waterlily varieties.

# HARDY WATERLILIES

In the following descriptions the water depth indicated refers to the depth of water over the crown of the plant. The approximate spreads are: small – 1–2 ft (0.3–0.6 m); medium – 2–4 ft (0.6–1.2 m); large – 4–8 ft (1.2–2.4 m).

## Red Varieties

*Varieties suitable for water 6–9 in (15–23 cm) deep*

'Ellisiana' An ideal variety for tubs or small pools where brilliant red flowers are required. Raised by Marliac in 1896 and achieving an Award of Merit the next year, it is easy to grow and reliable in its flowering. The flowers intensify in colour from a pinky mauve to red, and the centre petals sit upright while the sepals remain flat. They are about $3\frac{1}{2}$ in (9 cm) in diameter and are enhanced by attractive yellow stamens emerging from the purple bases of the petals. The small pads turn mid-green with age.

Approximate spread: small to medium

'Froebeli' This variety was the result of painstaking selection and breeding by Otto Froebel in Zurich, Switzerland. The fragrant and plentiful blood-red flowers are cup-shaped and are often held just above the water. The bright vermilion stamens bear yellow anthers, creating a truly stunning composition. A most popular variety, offering reliability and a free-flowering habit. A classic plant for the tub or small pool, it flowers well into the autumn.

Approximate spread: small to medium

'Laydekeri Fulgens' Another good example of the Laydekeri hybrids' habit of combining generous flowering with restrained leaf growth which makes them so suitable for tubs and small pools. This has vivid crimson to magenta flowers with fiery red stamens, and the attractive sepals are rose-coloured with dark green exteriors. The dark green leaves have an area of chocolate speckling around the leaf stalk.

Approximate spread: small to medium

'Laydekeri Purpurata' The star-shaped flowers are a crimson-red, and the strongly pointed petals, which are slightly spotted and flecked with white, surround bright orange stamens. They are prolifically produced, with several blooms appearing simultaneously from early spring until the autumn frosts. The comparatively small leaves bear maroon markings on the surface and are purplish underneath. Like most of the Laydekeri hybrids, they are suited to tub culture.

Approximate spread: small to medium

'Louise' Introduced in 1962 by crossing such good parents as 'Escarboucle' and 'Mrs C. W. Thomas' and patented in the U.S., this variety has delightful cup-shaped, double, deep red flowers with white-tipped petals. It has brownish-green sepals and yellow stamens. The flowers are held slightly above the water, and the mid-green foliage has slightly bronzed undersides.

Approximate spread: medium

*N. pygmaea* 'Rubra' Probably a natural hybrid, this variety is a true miniature for very small bowls and tubs, although it is slightly larger than many of the other *pygmaea* types. The tiny flowers, about $2\frac{1}{2}$ in (6 cm) in diameter, open dark pink or rose. The outer petals are white blushed with pink, and with age they become a rich maroon-red with orange stamens. The foliage is a plain green with a reddish undersurface. It tends not to spread even when it has the opportunity, making it particularly suitable for confined spaces. It is not the easiest of varieties to propagate.

Approximate spread: small

*Varieties suitable for water 9–18 in (23–46 cm) deep*

'Gloriosa' A great favourite with American waterlily enthusiasts, one U. S. catalogue describing its virtues as 'so exceedingly glorious that we recommend it as the basis of every collection'. It certainly is a strong challenger for the most popular red variety. The large, brilliant flowers, 6–7 in (15–18 cm) in diameter, are a light crimson colour, which deepens as the blooms age. It is very similar in flower to 'Escarboucle' (see below) but is not so strong growing. The reddish-orange stamens are held in fragrant semi-double blooms, which are, in turn, surrounded by five striking sepals. The variety was raised by Marliac in 1896, and two years later it gained an Award of Merit. The ability to tolerate light shade is an additional bonus to this variety with its dull, round bronzy-green leaves and adaptability to different environments.

Approximate spread: medium

Opposite above: 'Ellisiana'; opposite below: 'Froebeli'

Opposite above: *N. pygmaea* 'Rubra'; opposite below: 'Gloriosa'

'James Brydon' Achieving an Award of Merit when first shown in England by the famous nurseryman Amos Perry in 1906, this variety was developed by the Dreers Nurseries of Philadelphia and awarded a Silver Medal by the Massachusetts Horticultural Society in 1899. It is deservedly one of the most popular of all waterlilies. In addition to its many aesthetic attributes, it will tolerate a degree of shade. Its freely produced and distinctive goblet-like flowers are difficult to categorize as the outer petals are a deep pink, which shades to a rich carmine-red on the inner petals. These unique blossoms are 5–6 in (13–15 cm) in diameter, with orange stamens tipped with yellow. The broad concave petals are incurving, and they have almost a metallic sheen on their outsides. The fragrant flowers are perfectly complemented by the circular bronze to dark green foliage, which is often flecked with maroon. The freely branching rootstock will tolerate a wide range of water depths, from tubs to natural and extensive pools.

Approximate spread: medium

'Lucida' A Marliac hybrid developed in 1894, the rosy-pink, star-shaped flowers contain beautiful orange stamens. The flower colour intensifies towards the centre, particularly as the flower gets older, to a rose-vermilion. The outer petals and sepals are white flushed with pink. The leaves are an attractive feature of this variety: they have a deep purple mottling at the centre of the leaf, which becomes paler at the outsides. The leaves have very long stalks – even in shallow water they can grow to 6 ft (1.8 m).

Approximate spread: medium to large

'Sirius' Introduced by Marliac in 1913, flowers are almost as dark as those of 'Atropurpurea' (see below), and the deep rosy-red stamens are almost identical in colour to the petals. The sepals are also attractive, with red splashes on a whitish background. The medium-sized leaves are pointed, and they have a subdued bronze mottling.

Approximate spread: medium

'Splendida' ('Splendide') One of the more free-flowering of the red varieties, it was introduced by Marliac in 1909. The ruby-red flowers, which darken with age, have orange stamens. The foliage is a dull green, and its growth makes it a suitable variety for small to medium ponds.

Approximate spread: small to medium

'James Brydon'

Opposite above: 'Lucida'; opposite below: 'Sirius'

*Varieties suitable for water 9–24 in (23–60 cm) deep*

'Atropurpurea' A Marliac hybrid developed in 1901, it gained an Award of Merit in 1906. One of the deepest red varieties, the petals are a very intense shade of crimson. The flowers are flat, 7 in (18 cm) in diameter, with conspicuous yellow stamens with red bases but whiter on the tips. The young leaves are dark red, turning dark green with age.

    Approximate spread: medium to large

'Conqueror' Raised by Marliac in 1910, it received an Award of Merit in 1912 and is an extremely attractive, free-flowering crimson variety. The large, cup-shaped and incurving petals are flecked with white, and the numerous long, bright yellow stamens darken at the base. The sepals are striking, having white interiors, and the compact young foliage is purple in growth, changing to green with age.

    Approximate spread: medium to large

'Escarboucle' ('Aflame') One of the most outstanding varieties of waterlily because of its colour, reliability and vigour, it was developed by Marliac in 1909. The large star-like blooms are an intense vermilion-crimson, which deepens in intensity as the flowers age. The blooms are produced in quantity, some reaching nearly 10 in (25 cm) across. The fragrant crimson petals, which have a rich, spicy odour, contrast perfectly with the golden-yellow tips to the reddish stamens. The flower buds frequently emerge from under a leaf, pushing the leaf from the water. The coppery young leaves turn mid-green with age. It performs best when given plenty of space.

    Approximate spread: medium to large

'Newton' Developed by Marliac in 1910, this variety has brilliant vermilion flowers with unusually long, bright orange stamens. The flowers stand well above the water, the long, pointed petals creating a star-like appearance.

    Approximate spread: medium to large

'René Gérard' A very free-flowering hybrid developed by Marliac in 1914. The large rose-pink flowers are star-shaped and have yellow stamens. The flowers are 9 in (23 cm) in diameter, with the broad pointed petals a deep pink at the centre, where they are blotched and striped with deep crimson. The outer petals are paler. The glossy leaves are plain green with coppery-

Top right: 'Atropurpurea'; centre: 'Conqueror'; right: 'Escarboucle'

coloured undersides, and there is a pronounced V at the base of the leaf.

Approximate spread: medium to large

'Vésuve' ('Vesuvius') A prolific bloomer, introduced by Marliac in 1906, with flowers 6–7 in (15–18 cm) in diameter. The crinkled petals and stamens are both deep red, with yellow tips on the stamens. The young leaves are particularly attractive, with chocolate mottling on dark red leaf blades, which turn green as they grow older.

Approximate spread: small to medium

'William Falconer' A variety similar to 'Atropurpurea' (see above) but with cup-like rather than saucer-like flowers. The variety was developed by Dreers Nurseries in Philadelphia around the turn of the century and was named after a curator of the Botanic Gardens in Cambridge, Massachusetts. The foliage is dark purple with red veining, changing with age to green. The flowers, with yellow centres, are very dark red, 6 in

Opposite above: 'Vésuve'; opposite below: 'William Falconer'

(15 cm) in diameter, bearing stamens that are almost orange-red.

Approximate spread: medium

*Varieties suitable for water 15–36 in (38–90 cm) deep*
'Attraction' This is an attractive variety for large pools, where it needs all the space it can get. The flowers, 8–10 in (20–25 cm) in diameter, have rich mahogany-coloured stamens contained in garnet-red petals, slightly flecked with white, which deepen with age to deep red. The sepals are white with tracings of rose. The large leaves are bronze, turning to mid-green with time. Descriptions can vary, for the flower colour becomes deeper and more striking as the plant matures. Raised by Marliac in 1910, it achieved an Award of Merit in 1912. It probably deserves pride of place for the best

'René Gérard'

red variety for large pools and ranks among the world's greatest waterlilies. It is one of the few lilies that will grow in 3 ft (0.9 m) of water.

Approximate spread: medium to large

'Charles de Meurville' An exceptionally free-flowering and extremely vigorous variety, it is one of the first to flower, producing several plum-coloured 10 in (25 cm) blooms, which are streaked with white, from early May. Its huge leaves are slightly pointed and shaped rather like Nuphar leaves. They are a handsome olive colour, similar to 'Conqueror' (see above) but without the slightly rippled edge to the leaf. It is a Marliac introduction, from c. 1930.

Approximate spread: medium to large

'Rembrandt' The large flowers of this variety are a maroon-red colour with a pink flush on the outer petals. The leaves, also large, are roundish in shape and a coppery colour. It is a vigorous variety for the larger pool where its growth is not constrained.

Approximate spread: medium to large

'Sultan' Introduced by Marliac in 1910, this variety carries large, cup-shaped, cherry-red blossoms. The petals are tipped and flecked with white, and they darken towards the base. It is a prolific bloomer and vigorous grower.

Approximate spread: large

### Pink Varieties
*Varieties suitable for water 6–12 in (15–30 cm) deep*
'Laydekeri Lilacea' A free-flowering variety of fragrant cup-shaped flowers, which, despite the name, are more of a soft-rose colour than lilac. They later deepen to a rose and crimson. The blossom, which is about $2\frac{1}{2}$ in (6 cm) in diameter, is enclosed by dark green, rose-edged sepals and contains bright yellow stamens. There are slight brown markings on otherwise uniformly green leaves. It is a popular variety for tub cultivation.

Approximate spread: small

'Mary Patricia' A U.S. variety, which is suitable for small ponds or tub cultivation. It produces most attractive cup-shaped pink and peach-blossom flowers with great freedom.

Approximate spread: small

'Pink Opal' Another U.S. variety, this produces delicate pink flowers, which are held nearly 9 in (23 cm) above the water surface and which can be used for cutting.

Top left: 'Attraction'; centre: 'Charles de Meurville'; left: 'Rembrandt'

The flower buds are almost completely round and coral-pink in colour. It makes an ideal subject for tubs and, despite its delicate appearance, is easy to grow.

Approximate spread: small to medium

'Rose Magnolia' (*N. tuberosa* var. *rosea*) A U.S. hybrid with goblet-shaped pale pink flowers with yellow stamens. The long, heart-shaped bronze leaves, which have a wide indentation at the base, turn green with age. The leaves frequently overlap, and they tend to fold up at the margins like those of a Victoria.

Approximate spread: small

'Somptuosa' A good variety for growing in containers. The deliciously scented and large double pink flowers, 5 in (13 cm) in diameter, are cup-shaped. They are produced early in the season and contain vivid orange stamens, which contrast with the rose-pink, velvety petals that deepen in colour towards the centre. Introduced by Marliac in 1909, it has compact growth.

Approximate spread: small to medium

'Sultan'

'Laydekeri Lilacea'

*Varieties suitable for water 9–18 in (23–46 cm) deep*

'Brackleyi Rosea' A popular, vigorous variety, this waterlily was originated from plants grown by the Rev. J. H. Brakeley of Bordentown, New Jersey, and introduced by Sturtevant in Hollywood, California, before 1907. The fragrant rose-pink flowers, which contain golden stamens, are held above the water surface. The pink pales almost to white as the flower matures. The brittle leaves are deep green.

Approximate spread: medium to large

'Firecrest' A U.S. hybrid of odorata origin with a name that amply describes its unique appearance. The distinctive stamens, which are bright orange with red tips, stand erect in the centre of the dish-like flower of flat pink petals. The strongly scented flowers, which open early in the spring, are surrounded by purplish leaves.

Approximate spread: small to medium

'Helen Fowler' An American introduction by Shaw, this natural cross is one of the better selections of the *odorata* types. It holds its large fragrant flowers, which are an exquisite shade of rich pink, well above the water. The leaves, which have the typically circular shape of *odorata* hybrids, are soft green and not too demanding in space. It is a good variety for tubs or small pools, but it is becoming increasingly difficult to obtain.

Approximate spread: small to medium

'Lustrous' This variety of American origin is popular although it is of only limited availability. The prolific and beautiful cup-shaped flowers have broad, soft pink petals with a velvety satin texture, and they contain a bright cluster of thick canary-yellow stamens. The sepals have a pink interior with brown undersides. The young leaves are a copper colour turning to dark green with age. It is one of the few hardy hybrids to set seed.

Approximate spread: small to medium

'Odalisque' Introduced by Marliac in 1908, this variety is sometimes listed as 'Opalisque'. It is becoming difficult to obtain, although it is still listed in the Marliac catalogue. The rhizomatous rootstocks are one of the clues to its having the species *tuberosa* in its pedigree. A very beautiful variety, the prolific, soft pink, star-like blooms change to rose with age. The flowers, with their bright golden stamens and reflexed sepals, are held above the water.

Approximate spread: small to medium

'Rose Arey' A U.S. waterlily raised by Mrs Helen Fowler in 1913 as part of the breeding programme at her family's waterlily farm in Kenilworth near Washington,

D. C. Named after her cousin, it received an Award of Merit in 1937 and has been described as a connoisseur's variety. It has large, stellate, rose-pink flowers, 8 in (20 cm) in diameter, with fragrant, narrow, incurving petals, which have a tendency to curl. The brilliant orange stamens are tipped with yellow. The very attractive rich purple foliage changes to green with age. It is one of the best rose-pink varieties to be recommended for small ponds. Allow longer than most varieties for it to become properly established and it will become a reliable and free-flowering beauty.

Approximate spread: small to medium

*Varieties adaptable to water 9–24 in (23–60 cm) deep*

'American Star' Developed by Perry Slocum and introduced to commerce in 1985, this vigorous, free-flowering and striking variety has large, star-like flowers with narrow pointed petals. The petals are pale pink, deeper at the bases and fading to almost white at the tips. The stamens are a lemon-yellow colour. The young leaves are purple, turning later to green with purple undersides.

Approximate spread: small to medium

'Arethusa' A beautiful variety and one whose origins have been veiled. Available in Britain since before 1908, Marliac attributed its origin to Dreer in his 1922 catalogue. The flowers, which are similar to those of 'James Brydon' (see page 53), are large and in the shape of a wide, shallow bowl with salmon-pink petals flushed with a darker rose pink. The striking golden stamens provide a superb contrast.

Approximate spread: small to medium

'Eugene de Land' ('Eugenia de Land') One of the best of the *odorata* hybrids with its large, 7–8 in (17–20 cm) in diameter, scented semi-double, rich pink flowers. The golden-yellow stamens are surrounded by long, pointed flesh-coloured incurved petals, giving a star-like shape to the flower, which are often held above the water. Allow plenty of room to grow as a group.

Approximate spread: small to medium

'Fabiola' A Marliac hybrid developed in 1913. It has a good reputation for being vigorous and free-flowering. The large, rich pink flowers, which have brown stamens, are produced over a long season in generous quantity.

Approximate spread: small to medium

'Mme Wilfron Gonnêre' This outstanding variety is a Marliac introduction and one of few to bear double

Opposite above: 'Firecrest': opposite below: 'Arethusa'

'Eugene de Land'

'Fabiola'

flowers. The pink blooms are shaped like a deep bowl with yellow centres. The pointed petals are a very soft pink, almost white, with a deeper shade of pink nearer the centre, and green sepals. The flowers, sitting on a backcloth of mid-green foliage, have been likened to camellias. The leaves are unusual in having no distinct V-shaped gap at the junction of the leaf stalk, the leaf bases overlapping instead.

Approximate spread: medium to large

'Masaniello' The vigorously scented and free-flowering rose-pink, paeony-shaped flowers are exceptionally large and held above the water surface. The white sepals and amber stamens accent the carmine-dotted, rose-coloured petals, which intensify to a deep carmine with age. It was introduced by Marliac in 1908 and is more tolerant of shade than most.

Approximate spread: medium to large

*N. odorata* var. *rosea* A North American species that is sometimes called the Cape Cod pond waterlily or the

Boston lily after one of the areas in which it was found growing naturally. It bears medium-sized flowers, 3–4 in (8–10 cm) in diameter, which are one of the most fragrant of all waterlilies. They are a delicate soft pink colour, which intensifies towards the centre. It has a unique habit of maintaining the sepals in a horizontal position after the opening of the bloom. The stamens are yellow, and the leaves are brown when young, but turn green on the upper surface with age. It seeds freely, and old flowers should be removed to prolong the flowering season. It received an Award of Merit in 1895 and a First Class Certificate in 1898 after its introduction into the U.K. in 1881. It is at home in the margins of very large pools where it has room to develop in the shallow regions. This desire for space makes it more of a collector's item than an ideal variety for small to medium-sized pools. It is interesting historically for it was discovered in the United States in the soil of a low-lying valley on ground that had been recently ploughed. When it was found that these tubers were beautiful pink waterlilies, they were introduced into

'Mme Wilfron Gonnêre'

'Masaniello'

cultivation and were the source of the present commercial stocks. All the American odorata hybrids have proved to be capable of surviving in dried-up ponds. *N. odorata* var. *rosea* has given rise to many new varieties.

Approximate spread: medium to large

'Pearl of the Pool' Raised by Perry Slocum in 1946, this was the first hardy waterlily to be patented in the United States. Like many of Perry Slocum's beautiful pink introductions, this variety has cup-shaped, bright pink flowers, 5–6 in (13–15 cm) in diameter. The flowers have long slender petals with deep yellow stamens. The leaves are rounded and are a coppery colour on the underside.

Approximate spread: medium to large

'Pink Sensation' Sensational is not too strong a word to describe this superb American waterlily, which was introduced by Perry Slocum in 1964. An unusual feature of this variety is its ability to remain open in the evening for several hours longer than most other varieties. The incredibly beautiful flowers are 8 in (20 cm) in diameter and fragrant, with long, silvery-pink oval shaped petals with deeper pink bases held above the water surface. The deep green leaves have reddish undersides. In the last two summers in the U. K. it has out-performed most other varieties in the sheer volume of flower production. It is a variety that is likely to have a great future, even under glass in Britain, where the temptation is, in general, to use the floriferous tropicals.

Approximate spread: medium to large

'William B. Shaw' An *odorata* hybrid, which provides a flower with a beautiful contrast of colour within the ring of petals. The blooms are cup-shaped, medium-sized, fragrant and held above the water on strong stalks. The delicate rose-pink flowers have a deeper coloration on the inside of the narrowly pointed petals. The variety was raised in America by Dreers Nurseries in honour of the distinguished waterlily grower at Kenilworth near Washington, D. C. It is a strong and prolific bloomer.

Approximate spread: medium

*Varieties suitable for water 12–30 in (30–76 cm) deep*
'Amabilis' ('Pink Marvel') This is a very beautiful variety, which was introduced by Marliac in 1921. It has large, flat, star-shaped flowers, 10 in (25 cm) across, in a very subtle light pink to salmon colour. The fine yellow stamens intensify to a fiery orange with age, as the deeply cut and pointed foliage also changes from dark red to olive green. It is another variety that can

hold its blooms open until evening. Ideally it should be given plenty of space to develop its full potential.

Approximate spread: medium to large

'Marliacea Carnea' Developed by Marliac in 1887, this variety is also known as 'Marliac Flesh' or 'Morning Glory'. In the first year after planting, the star-shaped flowers, which are 8 in (20 cm) in diameter, are almost white with golden-yellow stamens. Although with time they develop a deepening pink flush at the base of the flower, they appear to be white from a distance. It is an exceptionally vigorous and free-flowering variety and is therefore, one of the commonest of cultivated lilies. The large leaves turn from purple to deep green with age. It is equally at home in deep or shallow water.

Approximate spread: large

'Marliacea Rosea' This beautiful variety was the first of the coloured Marliac hybrids to be produced in 1879; in 1900 it received an Award of Merit. As with 'Marliacea Carnea', the flower colour may be initially disappointing, as it tends to develop a true deep rose shade only in later years. It could easily be confused with 'Carnea', but it has a deeper flush of rose at the centre of the large, cup-shaped flower. The foliage turns from purple to dark green with age. It is an outstandingly popular variety for the larger pool.

Approximate spread: medium to large

'Ray Davies' Introduced in 1986 by Perry Slocum and voted best new introduction by the International Water Lily Society during the third annual Symposium at the Denver Botanic Gardens, this beautiful waterlily, which is much like 'Gonnère' in blossom form, has large, double, pink flowers. The numerous, large, slightly incurved petals are pale pink on the inner sides, darkening slightly towards the base and almost white on the outer sides. The centre of the flower is a striking egg-yolk yellow composed of several yellow stamens. The foliage is glossy mid-green.

Approximate spread: medium

'Rosy Morn' One of the larger pink flowering varieties, it is not commonly seen but is available in the United States, where it was developed by Johnson in 1932. Its stellate, two-tone pink blooms are richly scented and held on strong stems. It is used as a cut flower.

Approximate spread: medium to large

'Turicensis' A delightful and delicate soft rose-pink flower, which is fragrant and quite similar to *N. odorata*

Opposite above: 'Pink Sensation'; opposite below: 'Amabilis'

'Marliacea Rosea'

var. *rosea*. It is tolerant of different water depths and is, therefore, a suitable variety for the edge of large pools.

Approximate spread: medium

*Varieties for water 15–36 in (38–90 cm) deep*
'Colossea' A Marliac hybrid introduced in 1901, this is an exceptionally vigorous variety, producing huge, pale flesh-pink flowers with yellow stamens from May to October. It is frequently listed as a white variety, as the large fragrant blooms, 8 in (20 cm) in diameter, quickly lose their pale pink coloration and turn white. The round, bronzy-green leaves have very long leaf stalks enabling them to grow in deep water. The plant's capacity for flowering is enormous, providing flowers well into cold autumn days, even in northern England.

Approximate spread: large

'Gloire du Temple sur Lot' So many waterlily growers have extolled the virtues of this waterlily and Marliac himself has described it as 'Queen of the waterlilies'. It is shy to flower in its early years, but when it does, it has a unique mass of narrow, incurved and wrinkled petals with yellow stamens resembling a large, double chrysanthemum flower. It is the palest of blush pinks on the first day, changing to almost pure white by the third day. It was introduced by Marliac in 1913 and named after his home. As a unique bloom and rarity, it is worth seeking out for the enthusiastic collector.

Approximate spread: medium

'Mrs C. W. Thomas' Named in honour of the breeder's mother, this variety was, in 1931, the first waterlily for which a patent was applied. It has large, fragrant, semi-double pink flowers. A vigorous grower, it is recommended for large pools.

Approximate spread: medium to large

'Mrs Richmond' A Marliac introduction, dating from 1910, this beautiful hybrid has very large, sweet-scented, cup-like flowers, 9 in (23 cm) in diameter. In 1911, it was given an Award of Merit, only a year after its introduction. The prolific flowers are pale rose pink on opening, deepening with age to deep crimson. The petals are broad, full and slightly incurved, giving the cup-like shape. The petal bases are bright red and surround very conspicuous golden stamens enclosed by white sepals. The leaves, which tend to ripple on the surface rather than sitting flat, are a very attractive light green.

Approximate spread: medium to large

Opposite: 'Ray Davies'

*N. tuberosa* var. *rosea* An exceptionally strong-growing variety, with very fragrant, medium-sized flowers, 4–5 in (10–13 cm) in diameter, which are soft pink and fragrant. The stamens are bright red. The abundant pale green leaves have longitudinal red stripes on the leaf stalks. The variety is demanding on space and is better, therefore, confined to containers. It will thrive best in deep water.

Approximate spread: medium to large

### White Varieties

*Varieties suitable for water 6–12 in (15–30 cm) deep*
*N. candida* A hardy species for shallow water, this has a wide distribution ranging across north Europe, Asia and to the Himalyas, making it a good choice for colder areas. It is similar in appearance to *N. pygmaea* 'Alba', but it has slightly larger flowers, which, on closer examination, have small red stigmas in contrast

Opposite above: 'Turicensis'; opposite below: 'Colossea'

'Gloire du Temple sur Lot'

to those of 'Alba', which are yellow. This break in the uniformity of the colouring makes it a pretty little species worth growing in small pools. The white flowers, which are held above the water, are cup-shaped, 3 in (8 cm) in diameter, and have sepals tinged with green. The basal lobes on the light green leaves overlap slightly, and there are prominent veins on the undersides.

Approximate spread: small

'Hermine' ('Hermione') Introduced by Marliac in 1910, the attractive, pure white, star-shaped flowers stand 3–4 in (8–10 cm) above the water on stiff stalks. The flowers, which are produced profusely over a long period, have outer sepals that are a bright emerald green, similar to the colour of the oval foliage. It is quite a versatile plant, and it will tolerate not only different sizes of container but also semi-shade.

Approximate spread: small to medium

Above: 'Mrs Richmond'; above right: *N. pygmaea* 'Alba'

'Lactea' A very graceful and free-flowering hybrid, which was developed in 1907. It is thought to be related to *N. odorata* because of its rich scent. When the flowers first open they are slightly tinged with an apricot colour, but this soon changes to pure white. The outer sepals are bright green. It is best suited to small, shallow pools.

Approximate spread: small to medium

*N. odorata minor* A pure white dwarf lily, which is found in shallow swamps in North America and is often referred to as the mill pond lily. It was introduced to Britain in 1812. It can be successfully grown in tubs or in shallow pools, but requires full sun. The small, sweetly scented flowers are star-shaped, 3 in (8 cm) in diameter, with brown stems, and are freely produced. The leaves, 3–4 in (8–10 cm) in diameter, have dark red undersides.

Approximate spread: small

*N. pygmaea* 'Alba' A species with wide distribution in many countries, particularly in the northern hemisphere, and it was introduced to Britain in 1805. Its common names include pygmy waterlily, small white waterlily, dwarf waterlily and Chinese pygmy waterlily, and it certainly is the miniature of the waterlily family. The smallest of the white varieties, it is ideal for tubs, sinks and shallow pools, even aquaria where there is enough light. The dainty star-like flowers, never much larger than 2 in (5 cm) in diameter, contain bright golden stamens. The leaves are also small, only 2–3 in (5–8 cm) in diameter, dark green with dull red undersides. The rootstock forms an erect rhizome, black in colour and covered in long hairs. It has the ability to propagate easily from seed. Although its natural distri-

bution suggests that it should be tolerant of cold water, it does best when covered with 8–9 in (20–23 cm) of water that is not too cold.

Approximate spread: small

*Varieties suitable for water 9–18 in (23–46 cm) deep*
'Albatross' In the same year that Marliac developed 'Hermine', 1910, he introduced this other white variety, which he called 'Albatross'. The gently cupped, snow-white flowers have distinctive narrow petals containing a cluster of golden anthers. A feature of the variety is the changing colour of the leaves, which start almost burgundy in colour, change to bronze, then to a deep green as they mature. The plant is suited to almost any size of pool.

Approximate spread: medium

'Loose' A good, free-flowering, white U.S. variety of unknown origin. The sweetly scented star-like flowers are held on stout stems almost 12 in (30 cm) above the water, in a similar fashion to the tropical waterlilies.

Approximate spread: medium

*Varieties suitable for water 9–24 in (23–60 cm) deep*
'Gonnêre' ('Crystal White') Marliac raised this superb double white in 1914. The U.S. name for the variety is 'Snowball', which more adequately describes its appearance. The flowers, 8–9 in (20–23 cm) in diameter, are paeony-shaped and snow-white. They have thick petals, golden-yellow anthers and outer olive-green sepals, which remain in good condition for a long period. The foliage tends not to be aggressive and is a lighter green than is seen in most waterlilies.

Approximate spread: small to medium

'Hal Miller' Named after a U.S. breeder, this variety closely resembles 'Sunrise', which is one of its parents.

It is a member of the family of large white varieties and is known to have a degree of tolerance to shade. A relatively recent introduction, it has rich creamy flowers, which are held well above the water surface.

Approximate spread: medium to large

*N. odorata* (*N. odorata alba*) Although catalogues may list *N. odorata alba*, there is so very little difference between them that the two may be treated as one species. It is widely distributed in the United States, where it is common in naturally occurring shallow ponds. It may also be seen flowering at the sides of ponds where the water level has dropped leaving the lily high and dry. It is the most fragrant of all the American aquatics, an asset that has been carried to the many progeny bred from the species. The freely produced flowers are cup-shaped, generally surface-floating and approximately 4 in (10 cm) in diameter. The mainly pointed petals are white, and the four sepals are green on the outside and purple inside. The flower stalks are a purplish colour but not streaked. The pale green leaves, which are purple when young, are leathery in texture and almost circular in shape, 6–12 in (15–30 cm) in diameter, with red undersides. The rootstocks lie horizontally on the soft bottom mud, which makes them easy to remove and replant. The roots are rhizomes, 1–2 in (2–5 cm) thick and often achieving nearly 3 ft (0.9 m) in length. They are whitish in colour with black hairs. It was introduced into Britain in 1786 and later used by Marliac as a parent to many of his hybrids. It is at its best in the shallow water at the edges of large pools where the rootstock can grow into the slightly deeper water.

Approximate spread: medium

*Varieties suitable for water 12–30 in (30–76 cm) deep*
'Caroliniana Nivea' Developed by Marliac in 1893, this hybrid has inherited many of the best characteristics of the *odorata* group. It has highly scented, large, double, white flowers with narrow petals and rich yellow

*N. odorata minor*

'Albatross'

stamens. The foliage is a pale green, not too aggressive for such a large-flowered hybrid. It is a reliable, free-flowering variety for a small to medium pool.

Approximate spread: small to medium

'Marliacea Albida' One of the old stalwarts among the varieties being raised by Marliac in 1880, it achieved an Award of Merit in 1887. A remarkably free-flowering, fragrant, white variety, which carries the 4–5 in (10–13 cm) flowers above the water surface. The long petals, which have a pale pink tinge, gradually shorten towards the centre where they merge with the golden yellow stamens. The conspicuous bronze green sepals also have a faint pink flush. The large, deep green leaves are tinged with brown at the edges and have purple undersides. The plants are among the most popular white waterlilies grown, but they are vigorous spreaders and spoilt if contained in small pools.

Approximate spread: medium

'Virginalis' Marliac produced this hybrid in 1910, believing it to be the largest white hardy variety in existence. It is an excellent variety, the beautiful, large, semi-double flowers being 12 in (30 cm) in diameter. The petals are broad, shell-shaped and slightly in-curved, with snow white sepals that are rose-tinged towards their bases. The foliage is green with a purple flush. It is one of both the earliest and the latest of waterlilies to flower, and although it is rather slow to become established in the pool, it is well worth waiting for.

Approximate spread: medium to large

'Virginia' A U.S. variety resulting from a cross between 'Sunrise' (a yellow variety) and 'Gladstoniana' (a white variety) by Charles Thomas in 1962. The flowers are delightful, 6–7 in (15–18 cm) in diameter and almost double. The petals are pure white, changing to yellow in the centre. The leaves are nearly circular, and 9 in

Opposite: 'Gonnêre'

Opposite above: *N. odorata*; opposite below:
'Caroliniana Nivea

(23 cm) in diameter; the upper side is green, the lower side red. It is free flowering over a long period.

Approximate spread: medium to large

*Varieties suitable for water 15–36 in (38–90 cm) deep*
'Gladstoniana' An American variety produced by Richardson of Lordstown, Ohio, in 1897; it won an Award of Merit in 1911. One of the most beautiful white varieties, having exceptionally large, fragrant blooms up to 10 in (25 cm) across, full of golden stamens and surrounded by sepals with touches of green. The flowers tend to be bowl-shaped. The large, dark green, circular leaves, nearly 18 in (46 cm) across, pale with age. They also tend to push out of the water, exposing leaf stalks that are marked with brown. This habit is largely remedied by planting in a minimum depth of 2 ft (0.6 m). This waterlily can be very vigorous.

Approximate spread: large

*N. alba* This is the indigenous species of Britain, which is further distributed over a wide area of Europe and Asia. It is mainly found in large lakes or slow-moving rivers in which less vigorous submerged aquatics or hybrid waterlilies would not have a chance of surviving. Although often planted in the shallower edges of large lakes, its vigorous roots are capable of spreading enormous distances and to greater depths, some even surviving in 4 ft (1.2 m) of water. It is a robust and hardy species, not really suitable for domestic pools. Its flowers are the largest of all native British flora. They are cup-shaped, snow-white and 4–5 in (10–13 cm) in diameter, containing yellow stamens surrounded by broad and somewhat concave petals, which are further surrounded by four greenish-brown sepals with white interiors. The fresh green leaves, which are red when young, hug the water. The rootstock which is a strong rhizome, is thick and often 6 ft (1.8 m) in length with long fine hairs. If this species is grown by choice, these

'Virginia'

vigorous roots should be broken up periodically to prevent the foliage from obscuring the flowers.

Approximate spread: large

*N. tuberosa* 'Richardsonii' A robust and vigorous variety developed by Richardson from the American native *N. tuberosa*, which is at home in large pools. Although it is not very free-flowering, it is one of the first to flower, and continues to produce intermittent blooms until late September. The large, globular and multi-petalled flowers, 6–8 in (15–20 cm) in diameter, have distinctive pea-green sepals and centres filled with pale lemon stamens. The leaves are pale green and the tips of the leaf overlap. It is only truly at home in lakes or in deep natural ponds, and it has to a large degree been superseded by new hybrids. On dull days the flowers are reluctant to open.

Approximate spread : large

### Yellow, Copper and Changeable Varieties

*Varieties suitable for water 6–12 in (15–30 cm) deep*
'Aurora' Introduced by Marliac in 1895, the name gives a clue to its characteristics. The changing flower colours range from the first day's blooms, which are yellow, to salmon-orange on the second day and finally, on the third day, to a rich ruby-red. Where the plant has become well established and several blossoms are being produced, it gives the impression that there is more than one variety. As with many of the yellow varieties, the leaves are mottled and marbled, and in this case both surfaces of the leaves are marked. It is particularly suitable for planting in shallow water and tubs as it combines restrained leaf growth with prolific flowers.

Approximate spread: small

'Graziella' Introduced by Marliac in 1904, the small flowers are an unusual shade of reddish-copper, which is enhanced by bright orange stamens. The light green foliage has handsome purple mottling. It is a very free-flowering, attractive little plant, which makes a very good variety for tubs.

Approximate spread: small to medium

*N. pygmaea* 'Helvola' Introduced by Marliac in 1879, this is an ideal variety for growing in a tub or small pool. It has dainty, star-shaped, canary-yellow flowers, no more than 2 in (5 cm) in diameter, which have orange stamens. They are produced in abundance throughout the summer. The tiny olive green leaves are only 5 in (13 cm) across and are attractively mottled with purple and brown markings. It is an extremely tough little character, flowering over a very long season and resilient to poor conditions.

Approximate spread: small

'Paul Hariot' Another Marliac hybrid with changeable flower colour, this was introduced in 1905. Like 'Aurora', the flowers open yellow but change with age to a darker coppery-red shade, particularly in the centre. The flowers are cup-shaped, 4 in (10 cm) in diameter, slightly fragrant and held above the water. Flower size and vigour is deceptively large and strong for such a limited spread of leaves, making it another good contender for tub cultivation. The foliage is green, attractively spotted with maroon.

Approximate spread: small

'Robinsonii' ('Robinsoniana') Introduced by Marliac in 1895 and named after the English gardener W. Robinson, it received an Award of Merit in 1896. The star-shaped flowers are 4–5 in (10–13 cm) in diameter, with petals that are reddish-orange towards the outside of the flower, shading to rich orange-yellow in the centre. The colours are rather similar to those of 'Paul Hariot' (see above) but with softer tints, and they tend to deepen with age. The leaves are dark green, speckled with brown on the upper surface, dark red underneath. A further identification aid is the distinctive crimped notch on the edge of the basal leaf lobes. It is a fussy plant, flowering only to its full potential in full sun and shallow water. It prefers small to medium-sized pools.

Approximate spread: small to medium

'Solfatare' Introduced by Marliac in 1906, this orange-shaded variety opens with pale creamy-yellow flowers flushed with rose but they become more reddish-orange with age. The flowers are 4 in (10 cm) in diameter, star-shaped and held above the water. The dark green foliage has maroon blotches on the upper surface. It likes shallow water and is suitable for tub cultivation.

Approximate spread: small

*Varieties suitable for water 9–18 in (23–46 cm) deep*
'Comanche' A Marliac introduction in 1908, this variety not only changes colour as it matures, but also exhibits colour variations in parts of the flower. The petals change from apricot-yellow to a rich coppery-red, while the outer petals remain yellow. The flower stalks are long and erect, so that the rainbow-like flowers are held above the surface of the water. The distinctive colours are enhanced by deep orange-red stamens and by the young foliage, which turns from purple to green as it ages. It is a prolific flower producer, suitable for medium-sized pools, provided it has an adequately large container for the hungry roots.

Approximate spread: small to medium

Opposite above: 'Gladstoniana'; opposite below: *N. tuberosa* 'Richardsonii'

Opposite above: *N. pygmaea* 'Helvola';
opposite below: 'Paul Hariot'

'Indiana' A Marliac hybrid, introduced in 1912, this is an outstanding free-flowering variety in this group of colour-changing plants. The small flowers, which have yellow anthers, change from peachy-pink to orange-red as they age. The olive-green leaves can develop quite long leaf stalks, and they are distinctly marked with bronzy mottling. 'Indiana' is ideally suited to small pools and tubs.

Approximate spread: small to medium

*N. odorata* 'Sulphurea Grandiflora' Marliac produced this variety in 1888 as an improved form of 'Sulphurea', which he bred nine years before. It was sufficiently improved to win an Award of Merit in 1898. A rather shy-blooming variety, it must be planted in fairly shallow water and in a sunny position. The stellate, multi-petalled flowers are sulphur-yellow in colour and stand well above the water. The leaves are marbled above with chocolate-coloured markings, and red-spotted underneath. The variety is sometimes erroneously sold as 'Sunrise', but it can be distinguished from this variety by the lack of hairs on the leaf stalks and undersides of the leaves.

Approximate spread: small to medium

'Sioux' Introduced by Marliac in 1908, this is another multi-coloured variety. On opening, the blooms are pale yellow, then they turn to deep orange and finally to a coppery-red. The flowers held erect on strong stalks, have pointed petals, which are delicately spotted and edged with red, surrounding deep yellow stamens. The beautiful foliage provides a further enrichment of colour; the bronze-green leaves are mottled with chocolate brown on the upper surface and a rust colour underneath. A medium grower that is suitable for small to medium-sized pools.

Approximate spread: medium

'Robinsonii'

Opposite: 'Comanche'

*Varieties suitable for water 9–24 in (23–60 cm) deep*
'Charlene Strawn' A beautiful and fragrant yellow variety, which was developed by Dr Kirk Strawn of Texas and named after his wife. The numerous pale lemon petals surround the long, deep yellow stamens, while the prolific flowers, which appear over a long season, sit well above the very attractive, glossy green leaves. The leaves themselves have faintly purple undersides.

Approximate spread: small to medium

'Moorei' ('Mooreana') It is a change to see a variety from Australia, and 'Moorei' was bred at the Adelaide Botanic Gardens in 1900; it received an Award of Merit in 1909. A pale lemon-yellow variety with large flowers, 6 in (15 cm) in diameter, and bright yellow stamens, it is similar to the popular and more vigorous 'Marliacea Chromatella' (see below) but is distinguished from it by the absence of red stripes on the leaf and flower stalks and less blotching on the leaves. The leaves of 'Moorei' are pale green and have rather irregularly sprinkled brown spots rather than blotches on the surface but are more distinctly marked on the undersides.

Approximate spread: medium to large

'Sunrise' A U.S. variety descended from the tuberosa species, this has undoubtedly one of the largest and most richly coloured flowers of all the yellow varieties. 'Sunrise' requires as much warmth and sunshine as possible to flower well in temperate conditions. The huge and fragrant golden blooms, 8–10 in (20–25 cm) in diameter, are enhanced by the golden yellow filaments and narrow curving petals, which stand well above the water surface on hairy stems. The leaves are green, occasionally blotched with brown, and they have reddish, hairy undersides with wavy leaf margins.

Approximate spread: large

*Varieties suitable for water 12–30 in (30–76 cm) deep*
'Marliacea Chromatella' One of the oldest and most dependable varieties, it was bred by Marliac in 1887 and achieved an Award of Merit in 1895. A very free-flowering variety, with large, soft canary-yellow flowers, 6 in (15 cm) in diameter, which stay open later in the day than most other varieties. The broad, incurved petals surround deep golden stamens, and the sepals are pale yellow flushed with pink. The attractive dark green foliage is conspicuously mottled and spotted with reddish-brown blotches. It is sometimes called 'Golden Cup', as the flowers sit on the surface in this

Below: 'Indiana'

'Sioux'

Opposite above: 'Charlene Strawn'; opposite below: 'Moorei'

fashion. It is extremely hardy, tolerant of shade and adaptable to varying sizes of pool provided it lives in water of a reasonable depth. The vigorous rootstocks require frequent division if the full flowering potential is to be achieved. It probably outsells all other yellow varieties, as nurserymen can promise reliability of performance and flowers from early June to October. This late-flowering characteristic may be attributed to its sub-tropical ancestry.

Approximate spread: medium to large

*Varieties suitable for water 15–36 in (38–90 cm) deep*
'Colonel A. J. Welch' Introduced by Marliac in 1901, this is one of the most vigorous waterlilies in cultivation but has been superseded by other yellow varieties. The canary-yellow flowers, raised just above the water surface, are sparsely produced in relation to the masses of faintly mottled leaves. It has been observed to reproduce viviparously from spent blossoms.

Approximate spread: large

'Marliacea Chromatella'

# TROPICAL WATERLILIES

The spread of a waterlily depends upon plant parentage, container size, soil nutrient content, temperature and available light. In the following descriptions, the approximate spreads are: small – 1–2 ft (0.3–0.6 m); medium – 2–4 ft (0.6–1.2 m); large – 4–8 ft (1.2–2.4 m). Except where otherwise noted, the depth of water over the crown of the waterlily should be 9–22 in (23–56 cm).

## Day Blooming
### White flowers
'Isabelle Pring' Developed by George Pring in 1941 and named after his daughter, this viviparous variety has large, fragrant, pure white flowers, 10 in (25 cm) in diameter, which are cup-shaped with golden stamens. The very large, light green leaves are relatively compact in growth and have reddish-brown flecks on the undersides. It is a very popular variety.

Spread: medium

'Janice Wood' A recently introduced white variety, developed by Jack Wood of California in 1984. The tips of the creamy-white petals are rounded with a flush of the palest mauve, rising from an egg-yolk yellow centre. The leaves are distinctive, having a deep maroon background to the vivid green-striped blotches, the reverse coloration to the usual leaf variegation. It is free-flowering throughout the season.

Spread: medium

'Louella G. Uber' A 1970 introduction from Van Ness Gardens, this attractive, fragrant variety has star-shaped blooms of long, tapering, pure white petals. The arrangement of the beautiful golden stamens resembles the Inca symbol for the Sun God as the colourful outer whorl of stamens nestles on the inner white petals when the flower is young. It flowers continuously throughout the summer and well into the evening, after most other day-blooming tropicals have closed.

Spread: medium to large; depth: 2 ft 6 in–3 ft 6 in (0.75–1 m)

'Marian Strawn' Developed by Dr Kirk Strawn in 1984, this variety has white blooms, 5 in (13 cm) in diameter, which are held well above the surface of the water. The numerous long petals emerge from a deep yellow centre to form an almost perfect star-shaped flower. The leaves

are forest green and gently speckled. It blooms profusely throughout the season.

Spread: medium to large

'Mrs George H. Pring' ('White Star') Developed by George Pring in 1922, this variety won the Silver Medal of the Society of American Florists in the same year. The fragrant flowers are large, on average 8–10 in (20–25 cm) in diameter, with numerous pointed petals, which give them a star-like appearance. The creamy-white petals contrast with the bright buttercup-yellow stamens, which are tipped with white. The leaves are gently speckled. Although the flowers and leaves are large, this variety can be planted into medium-sized pools.

Spread: medium to large

'Ted Uber' Developed by Martin Randig in honour of Ted Uber of Van Ness Gardens, this free-flowering variety has large fragrant, semi-double flowers with bright yellow centres held above the surface of the water. The gently rounded petals vary in size, and the deep green leaves have a pink flush.

Spread: medium to large; depth 1 ft 6 in–3 ft 6 in (46 cm–1 m)

### Yellow flowers
'African Gold' Developed by George Pring in 1941, this is a variety with an intense deep yellow flower with forest green leaves, slightly paler beneath. The medium-sized blooms are smaller than the very popular variety 'St Louis' (see below). It has small leaves and is not a vigorous grower.

Spread: small; depth 12–18 in (30–46 cm)

'Aviator Pring' Named after George Pring's son who was killed in World War II, this variety has prolific rich yellow flowers, which are cup-shaped and rise high above the water on stout flower stems. The toothed green leaves are mottled and have wavy margins.

Spread: medium to large

'Eldorado' ('City of Gold') A Martin Randig introduction, it has very large lemon-yellow, fragrant and almost double flowers. The leaves are oval, dark green and heavily speckled. It is one of the hardier tropicals.

Spread: medium

'St Louis' Developed by George Pring in 1932, this was the first yellow hybrid to be raised and was awarded the Henry Shaw Gold Medal the following year. The large, star-shaped, medium-yellow flowers are 10 in (25 cm) in diameter and display deeper yellow stamens. The pea-green leaves are oval, 18 in (46 cm) across, and speckled in a bronze shade. It was, in 1933, the first tropical waterlily to be patented in the United States. The plant adapts well to either tub culture or a large pool.

Spread: medium

'Trailblazer' In the same year that Martin Randig developed 'Yellow Dazzler' (see below) he introduced another vigorous yellow, which is a prolific bloomer. The star-shaped flowers, which are large and very fragrant, are a deep yellow shade and are held high above the water on stiff flower stalks. The handsome, fresh, deep green leaves have a pink undertone on the undersides.

Spread: medium

'Yellow Dazzler' Bred by Martin Randig in 1938, this is an outstanding free-flowering yellow variety. The huge, flat, dish-like, lemon-yellow, stellate double blooms are carried on stems 6 in (15 cm) above the water and are produced in abundance throughout the summer, remaining open to dusk each day. The rich green leaves are very large.

Spread: medium to large; depth: 1 ft 6 in–3 ft 6 in (46cm–1 m)

*Rosy-yellow/autumnal shades*
'Afterglow' Developed by Martin Randig in 1946, this bi-coloured variety has large, fragrant, peach-coloured, star-shaped flowers with yellow centres, which blend to pink then a burnished orange on the outer petals. The smallish leaves are fresh green with paler undersides. It is a strong grower, which will adapt to small or large pools.

Spread: medium to large

'Albert Greenberg' Raised by Dr Birdsey of the University of Miami, this variety was named after Albert Greenberg, 'the father of aquarium plants', of the Everglades Aquatics Nurseries in Tampa, Florida. It is a very colourful and exotic hybrid, with cup-shaped flowers whose petals vary through the shades of pink, yellow, gold and orange. It has handsome mottled foliage and will adapt to pools of different sizes.

Spread: small to large

Opposite above: 'Isabelle Pring'; opposite below: 'St Louis'

'Golden West' Developed by Martin Randig in 1936, the large and fragrant stellate flowers change with age from a peach-pink shade through to gold and apricot. They contain golden stamens. The blossoms are held 12 in (30 cm) above the water on strong flower stalks. The leaves have a purplish speckling.

Spread: medium to large

'Talisman' Developed by George Pring in 1941 and named after a red and yellow rose bearing the same varietal name, this variety has large stellate flowers of pale primrose heavily overlaid with bright pink. As the flowers mature, the primrose deepens and the pink shading spreads, producing a beautiful colour combination. The small, dark green leaves are flecked with purplish-brown markings when young and have a reddish shade beneath. It is strongly viviparous.

Spread: medium

*Purple flowers*
'Director George T. Moore' Developed by George Pring in 1941 and named after a Director of the Missouri Botanical Gardens in St Louis, this popular hybrid has one of the deepest purple flowers of all waterlilies. The large flowers, 8–10 in (20–25 cm) in diameter, have deep violet petals surrounding purple stamens, which are in complete contrast to the striking golden centres. The smallish leaves, 4–8 in (10–20 cm) in diameter, are prolifically produced, blotched with maroon or brown on the dark green upper surface and pale green flushed with purple on the undersides. It blooms freely in clusters of flowers throughout the season, and its compact habit of growth makes it possible for it to be grown in small pools, even in tubs.

Spread: small to medium

'Edward D. Uber' Introduced by the Van Ness Gardens in the United States in 1985, the deep green leaves, rather similar to a jade green, provide a good backcloth to the attractive purple flowers. The deep golden centre is surrounded by pleasant shades of pink, which deepen towards the outside to a rich purple. It is reputed to grow well in a variety of locations, including cool and shady pools. It is viviparous.

Spread: medium

'King of the Blues' Bred by Perry Slocum in 1955, this variety has navy blue flowers, 8 in (20 cm) in diameter. The stamens are also tipped with navy blue, and the sepals are a purplish-blue with maroon overtones. It is an easily propagated variety and suitable for a variety of pool sizes and positions. It is an excellent bloomer and very easy to grow.

Spread: medium

'Midnight' Developed by George Pring in 1941, this variety has small flowers, 6–7 in (15–18 cm) in diameter, deep purple in colour with small golden centres. It is unusual in that it has slightly crinkled, deep violet petals, which vary in size from very large to almost stamen length, making it easy to distinguish from other varieties. The stamens appear to be replaced by petals making a dark blue rosette in the centre. The small, dark green leaves are sparsely flecked on the surface with reddish-brown and purple underneath. Although it is sometimes seen growing in small pools or aquaria, this variety does not flourish under such conditions. It is very free flowering and will tolerate a degree of shade.

Spread: small

'Mrs Martin E. Randig' Not to be confused with the varietal named 'Mr Martin E. Randig', this variety has attractive, fragrant blossoms of deep purple with long tapering petals. The large, deep green leaves are lightly blotched with a reddish tinge on the underside. It blooms heavily for many months.

Spread: medium

'Panama Pacific' Introduced by William Tricker in 1914 in honour of the Panama Pacific Exposition being held at that time in the United States, this purple variety later achieved an Award of Merit. The flowers stand well above the water's surface, with the inner petals having a distinct shade of brilliant rose-purple shaded amaranth, while the outer petals are mottled and flushed with purple. The fragrant flowers turn to a more reddish-purple as they mature. The yellow stamens have violet anthers, and the leaves are bronze-green with reddish veins. The buds are also attractive, being a bronzy-green colour flecked with rust. It is strongly viviparous and, being hardier than most tropicals and a good winter bloomer under glass, a widely planted variety. It is tolerant of a degree of shade and is the most adaptable of tropical waterlilies.

Spread: small to large

'Royal Purple' ('Royale Purple') The flowers of this variety are a purplish-lilac colour with a velvety sheen to the petals. There is a pleasant fragrance to the blossoms, which are 6–8 in (15–20 cm) in diameter and which contain yellow stamens. It is a moderate grower that is especially suitable for tubs or small pools. It is viviparous.

Spread: small to medium

*Pink flowers*

'Castaliiflora' Developed by George Pring in 1913, this variety has fragrant, light pink flowers up to 8 in (20 cm) across. The numerous open petals rest on the surface of the water during the third and fourth day of blooming. The stamens are yellow with pink anthers. The leaves are green with serrated edges, delicately mottled on the surface with reddish-brown and infused with pink underneath.

Spread: medium

'Evelyn Randig' Introduced by Martin Randig in 1931, this is a variety whose foliage is as attractive as the flowers. A distinctive and popular variety, the large fragrant flowers are a warm magenta-rose colour and are held on strong stems above the beautiful dark green leaves, which are very strongly splashed and striped with a chestnut brown and purple. It flowers almost constantly throughout the season.

Spread: medium to large; depth: 15–27 in (38–69 cm)

'General Pershing' Introduced by George Pring in 1920, this variety was awarded a silver medal by the Society of American Florists in 1923. The large and profuse, highly scented flowers, 8–10 in (20–25 cm) in diameter, are held as much as 12 in (30 cm) above the water. The orchid-pink flowers have light pink insides to the sepals and yellow stamens, which are tipped with rose. The flowers stay open for 12 hours a day. The dark green buds as well as the leaves are striped with purple and spotted with red on the undersides. A great favourite, its vigorous and free-flowering habit will adapt to many pools.

Spread: medium to large

'Leading Lady' Produced by Martin Randig in 1938, this variety has fragrant, almost semi-double, peach-coloured flowers. The exceptional number of petals open flat and are held above the water. The leaves are large, oval, overlapping and scalloped around the edges. The flowers are reputed to stay open under artificial light.

Spread: medium to large; depth: 21–33 in (53–84 cm)

'Persian Lilac' Developed by George Pring in 1941, this variety has dense, almost semi-double flowers of lilac-pink. The moderately large, fragrant flowers have broad petals with a mass of golden stamens with pink tips as the centrepiece. The light green leaves are occasionally flecked with brown above and crimson below.

Spread: small to medium

'Pink Perfection' Developed by Joseph Ling, this variety has fragrant, deep pink flowers with numerous yellow stamens with pink tips. The green leaves are

Opposite: 'Afterglow'

heavily mottled with reddish-brown stripes like spokes of a wheel. It will tolerate a wide range of water depths.

Spread: medium to large; depth: 1 ft–3 ft 6 in (0.3–1 m)

'Pink Platter' Developed by George Pring in 1941, this variety has, as the name suggests, broad open blooms which are very wide and flat. The flowers are a deep rosy-pink, 8–10 in (20–25 cm) in diameter, with numerous long, narrow and tapering petals. The golden stamens have pink tips. The moderately sized, light green leaves are flecked with reddish-brown markings on the surface and have flushes of red on the light green undersides. It is a very strong plant and will tolerate a degree of shade. It is viviparous.

Spread: medium

'Pink Star' An old-established variety with soft pink flowers held as much as 12 in (30 cm) above the level of the water on strong leaf stalks. The star-like flowers have golden centres and are gently flushed with lavender. It has large, light green leaves.

Spread: medium to large

*Blue flowers*

'August Koch' Named and discovered by George Pring in 1922 and grown from seeds collected by August Koch of the Chicago Parks Department, this variety has fragrant, lavender-blue flowers, 7–8 in (18–20 cm) in diameter, held well above the water. The stamens are a rust colour, and the sepals are a purplish-lilac shade. The dark green leaves, 12–14 in (30–36 cm) across, are pinkish underneath. A viviparous variety, it is extremely versatile and suitable for small pools because of its compact habit of growth. It will bloom continuously throughout the year and, being able to tolerate a degree of shade, is suitable for an indoor pool.

Spread: small

'Bagdad' Developed by George Pring in 1941, this variety has wide, flat, purplish-blue flowers with gold centres. The blooms are held just above the level of the light green leaves, which are blotched with red and brown on the surface and have purple stripes on the dark green undersides. It is strongly viviparous. It was named 'Bagdad' because its colours reminded George Pring of a Persian rug.

Spread: medium to large; depth: 15–27 in (38–69 cm)

'Blue Beauty' ('Pennsylvania', 'Pulcherrima') Simultaneous breeding programmes by William Tricker and Henry Conard of the University of Pennsylvania resulted in this hybrid, which was introduced in 1897 and has since been a firm favourite. The deep blue flowers,

10–12 in (25–30 cm) in diameter, stand 6–8 in (15–20 cm) above the water surface. The stamens are yellow with violet anthers, and the sepals are marked with black dots and lines. The dark green leaves are up to 24 in (61 cm) across, with brown freckles above, are purplish green beneath, and have wavy margins and long, tapering lobes. It is free-blooming with a long flowering season and is tolerant of semi-shade.

Spread: medium to large

'Bob Trickett' Developed by Pring in 1949, this variety was named after an Englishman who worked with Pring at the Missouri Botanical Gardens in the development programme of waterlily hybrids. It has very large, cup-shaped blue flowers, with a yellow centre of blue-tipped, lemon-yellow stamens. The large green leaves are round, and the red undersides show distinct green veining. It is reputed to be an improvement on the large-flowering blue variety 'Mrs Edward Whitaker'.

Spread: medium to large

'Dauben' ('Daubenyana', 'Daubeniana', Dauben's waterlily, Madagascar aquarium lily, blue pygmy waterlily) A German hybrid, introduced by Dr Daubeny in 1863, which has subsequently received several awards. The small, delicate, fragrant blue flowers are seldom more than 2 in (5 cm) in diameter and have narrow petals, which are touched with green underneath, white sepals and lemon-yellow stamens. The leaves are heart-shaped, no more than 10 in (25 cm) across, brownish-green in colour, splashed with chocolate markings. It is strongly viviparous. An excellent variety for the tub or aquarium as it prefers shallow water and will tolerate a degree of shade, it is generous with its flowering, producing several blooms at the same time during the summer.

Spread: small; depth: 4–16 in (10–41 cm)

'Leopardess' Developed by Martin Randig in 1931, this fragrant, medium-sized variety has sapphire-blue flowers held high above dark green leaves, which are strongly blotched and striped with maroon and chocolate. It is an easy variety to grow, particularly for winter flowers in glasshouses or conservatories, where it can adapt to any size of container.

Spread: medium to large

'Margaret Mary' Produced and patented by George L. Thomas in 1964, this variety is an excellent plant for tubs or aquaria. The small, star-like blue flowers are 1 in (2 cm) in diameter and have golden yellow stamens. The dark green leaves, which are 2–3 in (5–8 cm) across, have light brown undersides. The flowers are produced almost all the year round in cycles of three months'

flowering followed by six weeks' rest. Its ability to flower well under artificial light makes it good for interior decoration. It is viviparous.

Spread: small; depth: 4–16 in (10–41 cm)

'Margaret Randig' Another Randig family hybrid, this was produced in 1939. Martin Randig is reputed to have considered this his greatest production. The large, fragrant flowers open somewhat flat to display the broad, sky-blue petals and blue-tipped stamens. The dark green leaves are heavily speckled with bronze markings. A very vigorous variety with a generous display of bloom, it will tolerate a degree of shade and is a suitable variety for winter display under glass.

Spread: large; depth: 9–27 in (23–69 cm)

*Nymphaea caerulea* (blue lotus of the Nile, Egyptian lotus) A species from north and central Africa, *N. caerulea* has beautiful sky-blue flowers, 3–6 in (8–15 cm) across, held high above the water. The narrow petals are pointed, light blue above, the lower

'Leopardess'

half a dull white. The sepals are greenish-white and thickly marked with black lines and dots. The yellow stamens are slender with blue anthers. The green leaves are rounded, 12–16 in (30–41 cm) across, slightly wavy at the base and without indentations along the edge. There are conspicuous deep purple spots on the purple-hued undersides of the leaves. The large rootstocks are eaten in parts of Africa. Although it is not as showy as some of the hybrid blue varieties, *N. caerulea* is nevertheless a prolific bloomer and easy to grow. It will tolerate quite cool conditions, and the seed germinates readily. It has been extensively used in hybridizing, a notable offspring being 'Blue Beauty' (see above). The common names are misleading in that it is not a true lotus, which are, botanically, nelumbos not nymphaeas.

Spread: medium

*Nymphaea capensis* (Cape blue waterlily, Cape waterlily) This popular and very beautiful species has fragrant, blue, star-like flowers, 6–8 in (15–20 cm) in diameter, with plain green sepals and yellow stamens. The large green leaves are rounded and wavy edged, with splashes and blotches of purple beneath. The flowers stand well when cut and provide a delicate scent like violet blossom. It is easy to grow, flowering freely and producing fertile seed readily. There are many varieties of *N. capensis* of varying shades; one variety worthy of note is *N. c. zanzibarensis*, which has blooms up to 12 in (30 cm) across and is a deeper blue.

Spread: medium

*Nymphaea stellata* (blue lotus of India) This species is very like *N. caerulea*. Although very difficult to tell apart, the purist may be able to spot the violet undersides and prominent green veins that are present on *N. stellata* but not on *N. caerulea*.

Spread: medium

'Pamela' Developed by August Koch in Chicago, 'Pamela' was introduced commercially in 1931. It has beautiful, large, sweet-scented, sky-blue flowers, 10–12 in (25–30 cm) in diameter. The flower is saucer-shaped, with broad petals held high above the water on long stalks. The surface of the green leaves has a chestnut-brown marbling. It is a large and very free-flowering variety, carrying five to six blooms regularly at the same time throughout its long flowering season.

Spread: medium to large

*Red flowers*

'American Beauty' Developed by George Pring in 1941, this variety is such a deep pink that it is included in the red section. The medium-sized flowers, 6–10 in (15–25 cm) across, have delicately shaped, plum-coloured petals surrounding lemon chrome centres. They are held high above the water. The large, bright green leaves are rounded with wavy margins, and they are reddish beneath with prominent green veins. It flowers continuously throughout the summer and will adapt to most sizes of pool.

Spread: medium; depth: 15–28 in (38–71 cm)

'Jack Wood' Raised by Jack Wood of California, his namesake variety has fragrant, rich raspberry-coloured flowers with golden centres surrounded by ruby-red stamens. These bright flowers are held above large leaves, which are lightly blotched with brown.

Spread: medium

'Rio Rita' Developed by George Pring in 1941, this variety has moderately large, deep amaranth-pink, almost red, flowers. The broad petals surround purple stamens that have a golden colour at the base. The dark

green leaves are small with reddish-brown flecks sparsely scattered on the surface and red beneath. It is weakly viviparous.

Spread: medium

## Night Blooming

*White flowers*

'Janice Ruth' This is a moderate growing variety that is sometimes used where dwarf or pygmy types are required. The flowers, which open flat, are pure white with yellow centres and are much larger than the pygmy forms. The leaves are dark green. It does well in small pools and tubs. This plant is rare in commerce.

Spread: small; depth: 6–12 in (15–31 cm)

'Juno' (*Nymphaea dentata* 'Superba') This variety has been developed from *Nymphaea dentata*, which is commonly called the white Nile lotus and is native to Egypt and parts of Africa. First offered for sale in 1906, it has remained a popular variety ever since. The large, fragrant, white flowers, 8–10 in (20–25 cm) in diameter, are held on hairy flower stalks. The numerous wide petals have a faint blush of pink and open flat. The stamens are saffron yellow in colour, and the sepals are white on the inner side with faint greenish-white streaks on the outside. The large leaves have toothed edges, dark green above and blotched brown underneath, with prominent leaf veins. If it is to flower well, the water temperature should be around 80°F (27°C). It is a profuse bloomer and unusual in that it can be accurately reproduced from seed.

Spread: medium to large

'Missouri' Developed by George Pring in 1932 and named after the Missouri Botanical Gardens, this variety has massive, pure white flowers, up to 15 in (38 cm) in diameter, which look superb at night held high above the water. The broad petals surround a crown of erect yellow stamens. The young leaves are coppery brown, but become deep green with dramatic mottling as they age, and have wavy margins. As this is one of the largest hybrid waterlilies and has a strong constitution, it needs a large container and regular feeding. It flowers better in warm, sunny summers, but it will produce blooms in the winter in warm water under glass if there is sufficient light.

Spread: medium to large; depth: 20–34 in (51–86 cm)

'Sir Galahad' Bred by Martin Randig, this is another variety in the family of beautiful large, white flowers that stand well out of the water. The striking, star-shaped flowers have crispy-white petals, which are large and gently tapering and surround a bright centre of golden stamens. The large leaves are shiny and round and have wavy edges. It is becoming a popular variety, as it not only produces more blooms than 'Missouri' but also ones that stay open through to mid-day.

Spread: medium to large

'Trudy Slocum' Bred by Perry Slocum in 1948, this variety produces long-lasting blooms prolifically. The large white petals surround a prominent cluster of golden stamens. The foliage is plain green.

Spread: medium

'Wood's White Knight' Developed by Jack Wood, this variety has beautiful, vanilla-white flowers with prominent golden stamens. The emerald green leaves are variegated underneath. It is a prolific flowerer.

Spread: medium to large

*Pink flowers*
'Mrs George C. Hitchcock' Developed by George Pring in 1926, this variety has large, soft-rose flowers held high above the water and displaying conspicuous dark-orange stamens. The wavy-edged, copper-green leaves are flecked with darker green above and purplish-brown beneath. It is a reliable grower and extravagant in blooming, the flowers sometimes continuing well into late autumn.

Spread: medium

'Sturtevant' ('Sturtevantii') Bred by E. D. Sturtevant in New Jersey in 1884, this is an old variety of great size, which remains popular for its beautiful bright pink cup-shaped flowers, 8–12 in (20–30 cm) in diameter. The flowers, which are very fragrant, are held high

above the water. The petals are broad with incurving, orange-brown stamens. The large leaves are over 12 in (30 cm) in diameter, bronzy-green to apple green in colour, with toothed and wavy margins. It needs hot sunny weather and feeding to reach perfection.

Spread: medium

*Rose-coloured flowers*
'Emily Grant Hutchings' Developed by George Pring in 1922 and named after the wife of the secretary of Tower Grove Park, which houses the Missouri Botanical Gardens, this is an extremely popular variety, which thrives best with ample feeding. The cup-shaped blooms, which stand well above the water surface, are 10–12 in (25–30 cm) in diameter and contain gently curving, pale coral-pink petals surrounding very dark red stamens, which become mahogany coloured with age. The sepals have a bronzed-crimson overlay. The brownish-green leaves have wavy margins and are much smaller than the other night bloomers. The flowers are often produced in generous clusters of distinctive colour and sharpness.

Spread: medium

'Maroon Beauty' Introduced by Perry Slocum in 1950, this variety has the popular combination in tropicals of deep maroon flowers with bronze-red foliage. The flowers are nearly 12 in (30 cm) in diameter, and the colour shade lies somewhere between varieties 'H. C. Haarstick' and 'Red Flare'. It is free flowering.

Spread: medium to large

'Missouri'

Opposite above: 'Mrs George C. Hitchcock'; opposite
below: 'Emily Grant Hutchings'

Above: 'Maroon Beauty'

'Rosa de Nocha' A Van Ness introduction, this variety has creamy-white flowers, with bright canary yellow centres, and delicate petals, which shade from vanilla to ruby rose at their tips. The large leaves are bright green, gently touched with the rose of the blooms.

Spread: medium

*Red flowers*

'Devoniensis' ('Devon', 'Devonshire') This very old hybrid was raised in 1851 by Joseph Paxton, head gardener to the Duke of Devonshire at Chatsworth in Derbyshire, and the variety was named in honour of the Duke. There is some doubt whether it was a new hybrid or simply a seedling of one of the parents, N. *rubra*, used in the cross. Hybrid or not, its raising is often referred to as the beginning of waterlily hybridization. The rosy-red flowers, 8–12 in (20–30 cm) across, are held high above the water on stiff flower stalks. The stamens are a rich red, surrounded by oval petals 4–4½ in (10–12 cm) long. The dark bronzy-green leaves have toothed edges.

Spread: large; depth: 15–27 in (38–69 cm)

'Frank Trelease' Developed by James Gurney in St Louis in 1900, this early variety has brilliant, glowing, deep crimson flowers, 8–10 in (20–25 cm) in diameter, with long narrow but blunt petals surrounding bright red stamens. The huge, dark coppery leaves, 15–18 in (37–45 cm) in diameter, are splashed with green underneath. It is a shy flowerer and has to be encouraged by good conditions to bloom adequately.

Spread: medium

Opposite: 'H. C. Haarstick'

'Red Flare'

'H. C. Haarstick' Developed in 1922 at the Missouri Botanical Gardens by James Gurney and named after one of the commissioners, this variety has enormous fragrant and brilliant red flowers, 10–12 in (25–30 cm) in diameter, which are held well above the water. The long, graceful, tapering petals surround red and golden stamens. The dark coppery-red leaves are 8–10 in (20–25 cm) in diameter and have wavy margins. The dramatically red flowers are produced consistently in great profusion, and the plants require a great deal of space in which to grow.

Spread: medium to large

'Mrs John A. Wood' Developed by Jack Wood, this variety has maroon-red, star-like flowers and reddish-maroon foliage. It is not unlike 'Red Flare' but the red is not quite as dark and the blooms are larger.

Spread: medium

'Red Flare' Developed by Martin Randig in 1938, this spectacular variety has fragrant vivid vermilion star-shaped flowers and deep maroon stamens, complemented by the red tinged foliage. It is an excellent bloomer and will produce blooms into the winter under glass.

Spread: medium

'Rubra Rosea' This is the most commonly cultivated form of the species N. *rubra*. The large blossoms have petals of a beautiful cinnabar red, with equally red stamens. The leaves are strikingly bronzed.

Spread: medium to large

# NELUMBOS – LOTUS

Few flowers are steeped in legend, symbolism and indiscriminate naming to quite the same extent as the lotus, and it may be helpful to begin by eliminating some of the more common references to lotus blossom that have nothing to do with this genus *Nelumbo*. It was certainly not *Nelumbos* that the Lotus Eaters enjoyed when they were sent by Odysseus to find water and food on an uncharted island and that resulted in their loss of memory and soporific state. This plant was the Jujube lotus, a tropical evergreen tree known botanically as *Zizyphus lotus*. Nor was it a *Nelumbo* that was described as the 'milk-giving lotus' by the Roman poet Virgil in the last century B.C.: this characteristic was attributed to the common bird's foot trefoil, *Lotus corniculatus*.

The most common and confusing references to the lotus that is not a *Nelumbo* are those from ancient Egypt. Although these references are nearer botanically to lotus than others, they refer to *Nymphaea caerulea*, a sky-blue, narrow-petalled tropical waterlily, and *Nymphaea lotus*, a white-petalled night-blooming species. This commonly cultivated blue species of tropical *Nymphaea* is frequently depicted on Egyptian murals, and the early writings all refer to the plant as a lotus flower. The true lotus or *Nelumbo*, which we now often refer to as the 'sacred lotus of the Nile' is the Asiatic species, *Nelumbo nucifera*, which was introduced to Egypt around the time of the Persian invasion in 523 B.C. This *Nelumbo* became a commonplace plant along the banks of the Nile as its seeds were ground to make a type of flour, which was added to milk and water to make loaves. It has now almost totally disappeared from Egypt, reinforcing the argument that it was not indigenous to that country in the first place.

With some of the confusion over their identity cleared, the lotus flowers described below belong to the two wild species of *Nelumbo*: one from the old world – the Asiatic species *Nelumbo nucifera* (sometimes referred to as *Nelumbo speciosa*) – and one species from the new world – the American species *Nelumbo lutea* (sometimes referred to as *Nelumbo pentapetala*).

## Nelumbo nucifera (speciosa)

Some of the other common names for this plant include East India lotus and sacred lotus. Its distribution ranges

Opposite: *Nelumbo roseum plenum*

through southern Asia, the Philippines, Japan, India and south to northern Australia. It is this species to which has accrued the wealth of fascinating stories and symbolism, much of which is associated with the Hindu and Buddhist religions.

In the Hindu religion the lotus is the centre of the universe. The flower represents the country, its leaves the surrounding cultures and countries. In the beginning, the flower arose from the navel of the Great God and at the centre sat Brahma. Brahma's role was to recreate the world after the great flood. In order to do this he used parts of the lotus. Within each person inheriting the earth has been the spirit of the lotus.

The flower is sacred to the Buddhists too. Buddha appeared on earth on the leaf of a lotus, and the plant followed the spread of Buddhism as far as Japan and China. It therefore has enormous symbolic value in decoration throughout India and the East, the plants being preserved in pools and rivers, and the flowers treated with great reverence. It symbolized to the Buddhist the most exalted position of man – his head held high, pure and undefiled in the sun, his feet rooted in the world of experience. To the practitioner of yoga, the lotus position is adopted in exercises by those striving to reach the highest level of consciousness – 'the thousand petalled lotus'. To the very early civilizations, the flower was an emblem of female beauty and fertility, a symbol of life itself.

There are many similarities in the symbolic associations of the lotus and the waterlily, the contrast of the flower to the muddy soil beneath being interpreted as beauty rising from filth and squalor, even as 'hope arising from chaos'. One of the most pleasing symbolic references to these water plants is found in 'its perennial nature and rise to faultless beauty rising from a miry environment [which] suggested to primitive man regeneration and purification'.

## Nelumbo lutea (pentapetala)

This other wild species is found in North America, from New York and southern Ontario south, throughout the eastern states to Florida and Texas, and into Central America, the West Indies, and Colombia. It has several common names including lotus lily, pondnuts, winkapin, water chinquapin and duck acorn. Like their close relatives from the Old World, the plants have been put to good use as a food crop, with the tuberous swellings on the roots as well as the seeds being used in cooking in some form.

The seeds of both species are famous for their length of viability. A Japanese paleobotanist found in peat deposits in Manchuria seeds that were estimated to be 1000 years old. He successfully germinated these in 1924.

The botanical description and cultivation of the two species have much in common; the following notes are relevant to both *Nelumbo nucifera* and *Nelumbo lutea*; where any important differences occur they are highlighted in the text.

The rootstock is a long tuberous rhizome, which creeps below the soil; its appearance could be likened to strings of frankfurter sausages or bananas. When the plants are thriving in ideal conditions, these 'chains' of rootstocks can grow for many metres, each section growing from the tip of the adjacent rhizome.

The first young leaves to be developed are round, flat and surface floating. They are soon followed by the adult leaves, supported by strong, cylindrical leaf stalks attached to the centre of the leaf. The young leaves are tightly rolled as they grow and form such a sharp point that they can pierce any of their own surface leaves as they thrust out of the water. These leaves reach heights ranging from 2–3 ft (60–90 cm) to 8 ft (2.4 m) depending on the variety. The round adult leaves are usually bluish-green, up to 3 ft (90 cm) across and slightly frilled at the edge. The leaves of *Nelumbo nucifera* (the Asian species) are usually slightly larger than the American form.

The leaves have a beautiful shape, rather like an inverted parasol or cone. A wax-like covering on their bluish surfaces keeps them entirely dry and causes droplets of water to merge and appear like large beads of mercury. When it is raining the water collects in the centre of the leaf until its weight causes the leaf to tilt over to expel the water.

The magnificent, large, showy flowers stand higher than the leaves, and, like waterlily flowers, they have a life expectancy of three or four days. The flowers of the American species (*Nelumbo lutea*) are approximately 8 in (20 cm) in diameter and sulphur-yellow in colour with dark yellow stamens. The Asiatic species (*Nelumbo nucifera*) has larger flowers, nearly 12 in (30 cm) across, yellow stamens and petals that are deep rose on opening but become paler with age. By the end of the third day the petals are almost creamy-white with a rosy-pink blush at the edges.

The flowers tend to stay open longer each day as the flower matures, until they gradually shed their petals to reveal a most attractive, funnel-shaped seed pod looking somewhat like the rose of a watering can. This pod is approximately 4 in (10 cm) in diameter, downy and yellow at first, later drying to a brown woody texture. It is particularly sought after as material for dried flower arrangements. The nut-like edible seeds are held in pits all over the broad surface of the pod, the characteristic that separates lotus botanically from waterlilies. There are many colour variants and beautiful varieties, particularly of the Asiatic species, and some of these are listed below.

## Cultivation

Compared with the superb lotus plants that flourish in North America, specimens grown in Britain must be very well looked after if they are to achieve anything like comparable vigour and bloom. It is not simply a matter of temperature. Lotus seem to love sunshine and require a high intensity of light and warmth to bake and ripen the rhizomes. The best lotus grow in warm, almost hot, mud, a condition nearly impossible to achieve naturally in Britain. As with the successful cultivation of many other plants, the art is to create conditions that are as near as possible to those in the plant's natural habitat. This makes lotus cultivation in Britain dependent on glasshouse protection, at least for the winter months if not for the whole year round. There must be little shading on the glasshouses to cut down sunlight, and a balanced feeding programme is essential to make up for the short season.

Lotus need a rich loam and a large container in which to grow; they also need plenty of space and no competition for light. The loam in the container should be at least 12 in (30 cm) deep, with a covering of 3–6 in (8–15 cm) of water if under glasshouse protection. They are ideally suited to tub or container growing in Britain, but they must be fed frequently throughout the growing season. In order to survive in the wild, the shallow, chain-like rhizomes develop additional anchor and feeder roots, which penetrate the mud quite deeply. This habit makes them extremely difficult to remove from shallow lakes and pools in the wild and is a good reason why they should be planted in containers from the start.

Once a suitable container or tub has been found and filled to within 5–6 in (13–15 cm) of the top with a good loam, a shallow depression should be scooped out to take the banana-shaped rootstock. The growing point is delicate and vulnerable, and great care must be taken when handling and planting the rhizome not to damage this in any way as the rest of the rootstock will rot without it. The rhizome is then lightly covered with soil, leaving the growing point just sticking out above the surface. If the container is to be submerged in a larger pool, a surface covering of coarse sand will be useful to prevent the soil from washing out into the

water. The container does not need to be submerged, provided it is waterproof and in a sunny, protected place with 2–3 in (5–8 cm) of water covering the surface of the compost throughout the summer.

During the growing season every effort should be made to compensate for any lack of sunshine by feeding with a compound fertilizer such as those recommended for waterlilies (pages 41–2). The fertilizer should contain the three important plant foods – nitrogen, phosphate and potash – and there are many proprietary mixtures available for use. Each large container should receive the equivalent of 2 oz (56 gm) of a compound fertilizer that is high in potash every two weeks during the growing season. Once the foliage shows signs of yellowing and dying down in the autumn, feeding can be stopped.

Watch for any pests on the foliage. Red spider mite and aphids can be particularly troublesome under glass. If no fish are present, there are several chemical controls available, but where there are fish, frogs or other pond life, take care to use only controls that are non-toxic.

*Nelumbo lutea*, the American lotus, is native to North and Central America, the West Indies and Colombia

Lotus can be grown outdoors for the summer in tubs and brought inside as soon as there is a danger of frost. Once inside, keep the compost moist but not saturated for the winter. Take care to position the tubs outside in a sunny and sheltered spot out of draughts and wind. Sharp, unexpected gusts of wind can make a sorry site of tender lotus leaves.

In addition to the two species *N. lutea* and *N. nucifera* discussed above, the following varieties and forms are recommended.

*White flowers*
*N. alba grandiflora* (may be listed as *N. grandiflora*) This variety has huge fragrant cup-shaped flowers, which are frequently larger than 12 in (30 cm) in diameter and held high above the large green leaves. Numerous golden stamens make the centrepiece to this popular variety.

Opposite: *Nelumbo alba grandiflora*

*N. alba striata* ('Empress') This is a strong growing and a striking variety, producing lovely fragrant and globular flowers, with edges that are beautifully striped and tipped a rosy-carmine colour.

'Angel Wings' Bred and patented by Perry D. Slocum, this variety has long fragrant blooms, 8–10 in (20–25 cm) in diameter, which are almost tulip-shaped. The inner petals are attractively rolled, and the flowers are held well above the leaves.

'Chawan Basu' This semi-dwarf variety is free flowering. The beautiful blossoms are edged with pink and it makes a good specimen for tub culture.

'Shiroman' A Japanese variety with large, fully double, globular flowers, which open cream faintly tinged with green and become snow white with age. When the plant is established, the flowers can be 12 in (30 cm) in diameter, and this is a good variety for cutting as the flower lasts well when the cut stem is cauterized.

*Pink and red flowers*
'Charles Thomas' Bred and patented by Perry D. Slocum, this is a dwarf pink variety. The flowers open medium pink on the first day, changing to a lavender pink as the flower matures. It is ideal for small pools and tubs.

'Maggie Belle Slocum' Bred and patented by Perry D. Slocum, this variety has beautiful, large, rich mauve flowers, 10–12 in (25–30 cm) in diameter. The inner petals are beautifully rolled. This lotus will adapt to tub culture.

'Momo Botan' This variety bears fully double, peony-like carmine-red flowers on small plants, with leaves 12–18 in (30–46 cm) in diameter. Bright yellow seed

'Momo Botan'

'Mrs Perry D. Slocum' seen (above) on the first day of opening and, opposite above and below, on the second and third days

heads protrude strikingly from the aging pods. It is suitable for small pools and tubs.

'Mrs Perry D. Slocum' Undoubtedly one of the most beautiful and spectacular lotus varieties in existence. The huge double flowers are often 12 in (30 cm) across

opening rose pink and passing to creamy yellow with each day. It was introduced in 1965 by Perry Slocum. It is a vigorous grower and requires plenty of space.

*Yellow flowers*
N. *flavescens* This is a form of the American lotus and was introduced by Marliac. It is a smaller variety than the native N. *lutea* and has a red spot on the base of each petal and the centre of each leaf. It is strongly scented and is a soft shade of lemon-yellow.

# TENDER AQUATICS

This section deals with plants that originated in tropical or sub-tropical areas around the globe, primarily southeast Asia and South America. The plants listed will adapt themselves to a wide range of conditions other than those of their native habitats, making them suitable for cultivation in sub-tropical pools, in a conservatory display or in a tub garden.

### Alocasia (elephant's ear)

This native to tropical Asia creates a dramatic focal point in the shallow-water margins of a sheltered warm-water pool. Having much the same appearance as Colocasia (taro, see page 110), Alocasia flourishes in bright filtered sun and organically rich soil and with regular fertilizing. The flowers of the plant resemble those of Zantedeschia (calla lily, see page 124). The tubers of these rhizomatous plants are edible. Many of the species of Alocasia that are cultivated exhibit striking coloration of foliage, including leaves with copper or purple tones or with white venation. Propagation is by division. The following two species are among the more readily available.

*A. macorrhiza* The large, bright green, arrow-shaped leaves of this plant can surpass 2 ft (61 cm) in length. They are borne on slightly arching stalks up to 5 ft (1.5 m) long. After flowering, red fruits form on the exposed flower stalk. The plant will retain its foliage to 29°F (1.7°C) and, in a deciduous state, will survive mild frosts. The plant will grow in very moist soil, or with up to 4 in (10 cm) of water over its crown.

*A. odora* This plant is very similar to *A. macorrhiza*, but somewhat less tolerant of cold. As the species name implies, the flowers of this plant are fragrant.

### Alternanthera philoxeroides (alligator weed)

A native to South America, this plant is believed to have been introduced into the United States, where it has naturalized in warmer areas, as ballast in cargo ships in the 1950s. The creeping stems of the plant spread profusely in a wide variety of conditions, growing in very damp soil or with up to 2 ft (61 cm) of water over the crown. They will grow in full sun or moderate shade, and they will tolerate brackish water to 30 per cent sea strength. The medium-green, elliptic leaves, which cover the stems, grow to be 2–5 in (5–13 cm) long

and $\frac{1}{4}-\frac{3}{4}$ in (5–20 mm) wide, with a distinct midrib. The stems of the plant will stand up to 18 in (46 cm) above the water's surface. Intermittently, the stems can be crowned with solitary white flowers $\frac{1}{2}$ in (1 cm) in diameter, creating the impression of a snowfall over the plant bed. Propagation is by division or by cuttings.

### Ammania

A genus of approximately 30 species of submerged aquatics, which are becoming more popular with aquarists interested in cultivating a wider range of

*Aponogeton crispus*

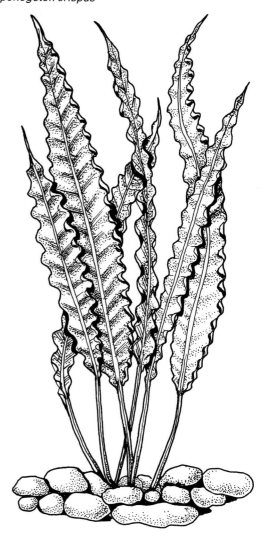

submerged plants. They are small plants that need plenty of light and a temperature of approximately 68–79°F (20–26°C). The leaves, 1–2 in (2–5 cm) long, are narrow and opposite on the stems, pale green to palish red. The flowers are small, stalkless and reddish in colour. The main species likely to be found is *A. senegalensis* from Africa. It is best planted as a small clump or bunch.

## Anubias (water aspidistra, African cryptocoryne)

Originating and becoming rare in west Africa, where it grows in shady bogs near tropical rivers, this species will withstand submerging for use in aquaria or grow emergent in terraria and tropical pools. Two species are commonly used for this purpose – *A. afzelii*, which has leaves that grow to 8 in (20 cm), and the smaller *A. nana*, with 4–6 in (10–15 cm) leaves. The plant has a thick creeping rhizome, which gives rise to dark green leathery leaves and small arum-like flowers. It requires a temperature around 75°F (24°C), and is slow growing at best. The rhizome of the plant should never be completely covered with soil.

## Aponogeton

Although the genus is renowned in Britain for the more common hardy species *A. distachyus*, the water hawthorn (see page 126), there are several tender species. Two are suitable for culture in temperate zone pools or in conservatories.

*A. crispus* (wavy-edged swordplant) This plant, which is sometimes confused with *A. undulatus*, is native to Sri Lanka. It is noteworthy for the crenelated margins of its 10 in (25 cm) long, reddish, strap-like leaves. It bears a white flower characteristic of the genus. Plants should be grown in tubs or in pools. The water temperature should be 70–75°F (21–24°C), falling to no lower than 50–60°F (10–15°C) in the winter. Ideally, the tub should be 3 ft (0.9 m) in diameter and 18 in (46 cm) deep. Good fibrous loam with a little charcoal added should be used, and the surface of the soil should be covered with gravel. The crown should be 2 in (5 cm) below the soil level, then covered by up to 12 in (31 cm) of water. If possible, use rain water and keep the water as clean as possible. Like all cultivated Aponogetons, *A. crispus* will adapt to bright or to subdued light.

*A. kraussianum (desertorum)* A native to Africa and Australia, this species has creamy-white flowers held 4–5 in (10–12 cm) above the water. Although hardy in some parts of Britain, the containers should be overwintered indoors. The leaves, like those of the common water hawthorn, are strap-like. The plants prefer shallow water, 4–9 in (10–23 cm) deep, in a sunny position. The best temperature range is between 68° and 80°F (20–28°C), dropping to no lower than 55°F (13°C) in water. Propagation is by seed.

## Bacopa (water hyssop)

A genus of approximately 100 species of submerged and emergent aquatics distributed worldwide but found mainly in America. They have a creeping habit with hairy stems and leaves, which are about 1 in (2 cm) long; the soft purple or blue flowers are ball-shaped. The two species most commonly grown are *B. amplexicaulis* (*B. caroliniana*) and *B. monniera* (baby tears), the former turning copper in bright light. They are best planted in clumps for effect and are easily propagated by cuttings, to be used as bog or marginal accents. They will accept a temperature range from 55° to 80°F (13°–28°C).

## Brasenia schreberi (water shield, target)

A tropical aquatic of widespread distribution including North and Central America, Africa, east Asia and Australia. The long trailing stems are capable of growing in 4–6 ft (1.2–1.8 m) of water in their native habitats. The small floating leaves, which have slimy undersides, are shield shaped and 2–3 in (5–8 cm) long. They are dark green on the surface with brown or red edges and reddish undersides. The flowers, which are drawn under the surface at night, are violet coloured, 1 in (2 cm) across and have three petals. They need 8–10 in (20–25 cm) depth of water, good light and moderate warmth. It is grown more as an oddity than for its beauty.

## Cabomba (fanwort, Washington grass)

A genus of approximately seven species of submerged perennial aquatics distributed throughout South America and the southern United States. One of the bettter underwater oxygenators for temperate pools, it is an attractive plant with wonderfully lacey fan-shaped leaves on a long, submerged stem. It can grow to over 12 in (30 cm) in height, with small white or yellow flowers $\frac{1}{2}$ in (12 mm) in diameter. It requires a temperature of between 64°F (18°C) and 77°F (25°C) in good light intensity and lime-free water. It is intolerant of water motion and is best grown as far away from any water movement caused by aeration or filtration. The two species mainly grown are *C. aquatica*, which has yellow flowers, and *C. caroliniana*, which has very tiny white flowers with two yellow spots at the base of each petal.

## Canna

Most species of canna are terrestrial plants associated with Victorian bedding schemes where the impressive foliage of the tall varieties gives a sub-tropical effect.

Aquatic cannas have been developed and are popular in America where warm, sunny conditions are more likely to prevail. They are similar in appearance to the terrestrial canna but have the ability to grow with their roots submerged in water. The species used in water is *Canna glauca*, a Brazilian plant with pale yellow flowers and erect narrow lanceolate leaves. Although this species flowers continuously throughout the summer, there are never a large number of flowers at any one time, and they do not present a striking display. A breeding programme was undertaken at the famous Longwood Gardens, Pennsylvania, to develop more floriferous and striking varieties, and four varieties are listed below that have limited availability in commerce. They are a distinct improvement on the original species and well worth growing in pools that are in full sun all day. The plants have thinner rhizomes than their terrestrial counterparts, and these should be planted in large tubs or containers such as those used for lotus or vigorous waterlilies. The compost should be very rich and the filled container should be covered with sand or gravel. Ideally they should be covered with 12 in (30 cm) of water. Given a good summer and frequent feeding as for waterlilies or lotus, they will continue flowering until the first frosts when they should be taken inside. They should then be placed into warm water and as light a position as possible for a winter under glass, when they will produce winter blooms. If there is no suitable heated space, they should be stored in damp sand or peat as recommended for lotus. The plants weaken under this treatment unless well fertilized, however, as they have limited food reserves in their thin rhizomes. In temperate zones these cannas may be overwintered in the garden pool. Their numbers may be increased by dividing the rhizomes in the spring. All four of the varieties that are listed below will grow to 5–6 ft (1.5–1.8 m) high; they have glaucous leaf blades that are nearly 2 ft (60 cm) long and approximately 6 in (15 cm) wide. 'Endeavour' has bright red flowers, 'Erebus' has salmon-pink flowers, 'Ra' has yellow flowers and 'Taney' has burnt orange flowers.

## Cardamine lyrata (bittercress, Japanese cress)

Originating in eastern Asia, this dainty little herbaceous plant with roundish or slightly kidney-shaped leaves, often with wavy margins, produces long white trailing roots and clusters of small white flowers $\frac{1}{5}$–$\frac{2}{5}$ in (5–10 mm) in diameter. It grows upwards of 8 in (20 cm). It prefers to grow at a temperature of 59–68°F (15–20°C) and in good light. It propagates easily by cuttings, and in marshy areas it has a creeping habit. *Cardamine lyrata* is a fragile plant that is susceptible to damage from water snails.

*Ceratopteris thalictroides*

## Ceratopteris

A genus of four species of floating or submerged succulent annual ferns with finely divided, long, dangling roots, which are ideal for small fish to breed in. It is found in tropical regions throughout the world. The juicy fronds are eaten in the East Indies as a vegetable. The plants need high light levels and a temperature of 68–77°F (20–25°C), and they do best in acid water.

*C. deltoides* The largest species has thick barren fronds, which are barely submerged, and fertile fronds, which are finely divided and erect in growth.

*C. pteridoides* A large rosette of pale green, wavy-margined barren fronds surround the taller and much divided fertile fronds, which stand erect in the centre of the plant.

Opposite above: Canna 'Erebus'; opposite below: Canna 'Ra'

*C. thalictroides* (water sprite, Indian fern) A water fern 21–30 in (50–70 cm) high above the water, with fragile pale-green fronds 18 in (46 cm) long and 10 in (25 cm) wide. Baby plantlets grow along the edges of the narrow fertile fronds and may be separated from the parent to form new plants.

## Colocasia

This genus of approximately seven species produces starchy edible rhizomes. The species are native to tropical Asia, but they are also grown in other Pacific islands including Hawaii, where their large leaves are widely used in decorative plantings. Some species have edible leaves.

*C. antiquorum* (Imperial taro) This species is much appreciated for its highly variegated, emerald green leaves, which are blotched with dark brown and violet

*Colocasia violacea*

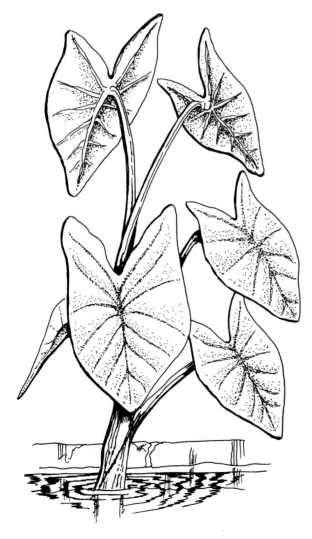

black, and it is used as an ornamental plant in temperate zone pools. It should be grown in rich soil in large pots standing in a few inches of water. It has thick stems, 3 ft 6 in (1 m) long, and long, heart-shaped leaves, 20 in (50 cm) in length with wide triangular bases. The arum-like flower is 6–14 in (15–35 cm) long, pale yellow in colour, with a green oblong tube and an unpleasant smell.

*C. esculenta* (elephant's ear, yam, taro) Another species with many varieties that are used for ornamental purposes. All have large quilted leaves, grey-green in colour, which grow up to 3 ft (0.9 m) long. The entire plant can grow up to 6 ft (1.8 m). The edible tuber, which is 3–16 in (8–41 cm) long and up to 8 in (20 cm) thick, is a popular vegetable in the West Indies and is used as a staple food in south China. It is propagated by seed or by division of the tubers, and it thrives in filtered sun in wind-protected locations. The most striking variety of *C. esculenta* is *C.e. fontanesii*, the violet-stemmed taro.

## Crinum americanum

This aquatic bulb from Florida makes a superb specimen plant. The pale green leaves, $1\frac{1}{4}$ in (3 cm) wide, may reach a length of 2 ft (0.6 m). The plant prefers a temperature of 68–77°F (20–25°C) with good light levels. Each flower stem bears from four to six flowers, which have white, spider-like petals. Planted in rich soil, it will stand 6 in (15 cm) of water over its crown. The best propagation results are obtained from the young bulblets, which develop from the base of the bulb.

## Cryptocoryne (water trumpet)

An interesting and decorative genus with about 50 known species; as more and more plants are discovered that number is steadily increasing. They are native to the Old World tropics and were first introduced into Europe in 1906. They flourish best in temperatures of 68–86°F (20–30°C), planted in river sand mixed with clay, peat or loam. Although tolerant of fairly low to medium light levels, they tend to produce their extraordinary arum-shaped flowers of many colours and shapes above water when more light is available. They have stiff leathery leaves of various shapes and shades of green. They take a long time to root and resent transplanting. Propagation is normally by division. The following species are usually available.

*C. lutea* This species has attractive oval leaves 4–8 in (10–20cm) long, with undulating edges. They are dark green on top, with reddish-brown veins on the paler green undersides.

Purple-leaved taro

C. *wendtii* This species was first named in 1958 and has since proved to be a popular decorative species. The purplish-brown to glossy green leaves with darker vein stripes are lance-shaped and 6–8 in (15–20 cm) long with corrugated edges. It is a fairly fast-growing species.

## Cyperus

An extremely large genus, which is widely distributed throughout the world in all climates except the cold. Some of the few species used for water gardens are described here. All will overwinter outdoors in temperate-zone pools or conservatories, but require winter protection in Britain.

C. *adenophorus* (C. *diffusus*, C. *elegans*, C. *laxus*) The plant's fibrous roots grow well in very damp soil or with up to 4 in (10 cm) of water over the crown. The many glossy, medium green leaves form a grassy mat up to 8 in (20 cm) high, out of which rise slender stems, 1–3 ft (30–90 cm) tall, topped by elegant, lacy flowering heads. The plant is much prized by flower arrangers. Although not the most dramatic, this is the most beautiful *Cyperus*. C. *adenophorus* is a tender tropical and will not tolerate cold below approximately 50°F (10°C), but it will thrive best in a sunny exposure.

C. *alternifolius* (umbrella grass) This species from Madagascar has ribbed stalks, 24–48 in (0.6–1.2 m) high, with a crown of bright green spikelets surrounding small green flowers. Two other forms of this species are worthy of note. C. *alternifolius gracilis* (C. *a. nanus*) is a dwarf type of the above with all parts smaller, including the very slender, wiry stems and narrow leaves, and growing to only 18 in (46 cm). An aggressive rhizomatous grower, it also readily self-seeds. It grows best in very damp soil or with up to 6 in (15 cm) of water over its crown. C. *alternifolius variegatus* is a form with shiny green and creamy-white banding that runs lengthwise on the stems and leaves creating a very attractive effect. This plant cannot be raised true from seed.

C. *haspan viviparus* This charming dwarf species from South Africa has slender triangular stalks, which terminate in small stiff crowns of ray-like leaves and reddish spikes, much like a miniature version of C. *papyrus*, growing to 12–18 in (30–46 cm). As the name implies, it is viviparous. Grow as for C. *alternifolius* in damp soil or with up to 2 in (15 cm) of water over its crown. C. *haspan viviparus* sometimes sold as C. *isocladus*.

*C. papyrus* (Egyptian paper reed) An extremely elegant and stately plant with strong, dark-green, triangular stems growing to 12–16 ft (3.6–4.8 m) high and crowned by brush-like umbels of pendulous, thread-like leaves. The pith-like tissues of the mature stems were used for making paper by the ancient Egyptians, and even today the stems are bound together to make rafts. It is likely that it was the bulrush plant in which the baby Moses was hidden from Herod in biblical lore. Along with Colocasia, this is the most dramatic accent or silhouette plant for a temperate pool or conservatory. Grow as for *C. alternifolius.*

*C. vegetus* (sweet galingale) This attractive species is fairly resistant to light frosts. It grows to 3–4 ft (0.9–1.2 m) high on triangular, stiff, smooth stems, which terminate in pendulous leafy umbels of pale green spikelets.

*Cyperus adenophorus* (also known as *C. diffusus*, *C. elegans* and *C. laxus*)

### Dichromena colorata (star grass)

This dainty native to Mexico and the southern United States prefers growing in very damp soil, but it will grow with up to 6 in (15 cm) of water over its crown. It has bright green, grassy foliage, 1–2 ft (31–61 cm) tall, and white, star-shaped blooms, 2 in (5 cm) in diameter, atop stems 1 ft (31 cm) high. The flowers continue through autumn, when the plant may go dormant and shed its foliage. Propagation is by division.

### Echinodorus

A fairly large genus including approximately 50 submerged species and closely resembling Sagittarias (see below). They are distributed from the southern part of North America through Central to South America. All the plants benefit from a resting period in the winter, but when in full growth, they need plenty of light, neutral water and a temperature of 65–77°F (18–25°C). The flowers are pure white and are arranged in whorls on a tall spike. At first the leaves are ribbon-like, but as they grow they become either heart-shaped or lance-like and are borne on long stems. They grow best in very damp soil or with up to 2 in (5 cm) of water over the crown of the plant.

*E. amazonicus (E. brevipedicellatus)* The long green, strap-like leaves, 10–20 in (25–50 cm) long, grow in rosettes resembling small bushes and are often bent with a predominant middle rib. Young plants grow from the base of the rosette. The inflorescence of this plant can be up to 40 in (1 m) tall. Many Echinodorus are sold as aquarium plants.

*E. berteroi* (cellophane plant) An interesting species of which the leaf shape varies as it develops. At first the leaves are slender and ribbon-shaped but they become broader and heart-shaped, 4–5 in (10–13 cm) long and 3–3½ in (8–9 cm) wide. They finally produce floating pale-green leaves with rounded arrow-shaped bases, which are a much tougher texture. This temperate-zone plant may be cultivated outdoors in a sheltered, sunny location in British summers.

*E. cordifolius (E. radicans)* One of the oldest cultivated species of the genus. The leaves of the very young plants tend to be egg-shaped, but they soon become heart-shaped, tough and pale green with prominent parallel veins and brownish translucent spots. The plant can grow 1–2 ft (31–61 cm) high, with taller flower spikes. Like *E. berteroi*, it will tolerate outdoor planting, with protection, in summer.

*E. tenellus* (pygmy-chain sword plant) Grass-like, this smallest of the Echinodorus forms low rosettes of

*Cyperus haspan viviparus*

narrow, dark green pointed leaves, 2–4 in (5–10 cm) long and about $\frac{1}{2}$ in (12 mm) wide. It is generally grown as an annual, and it forms an interesting mat of foliage. The flower spike is correspondingly small, but not insignificant.

## Egeria densa (Argentinian water weed)
This plant is an excellent submerged oxygenator much resembling *Elodea canadensis* in appearance, but slightly more tender. The narrow, dark-green leaves, 1 in (2 cm) long, are produced in whorls on branching stems of anything from 1 to 7 ft (30–200 cm). The white flowers, which are produced above water, have three petals.

## Eichhornia
There are seven species in this attractive tropical South American genus, and all produce eye-catching flowers if there is enough hot sunshine. They are generally propagated by cutting the young plants from runners off the parent plant. Because Eichhornia is such a rampant grower, restrictions on its importation or sale have been enacted in many temperate zones. Eichhornia species have been widely used as purifiers, their pendulous roots absorbing heavy metals from re-claimed water.

*E. azurea* (peacock hyacinth) Plenty of space is needed for this marginal plant, especially if the water is warm, because it can spread to 6 ft (1.8 m), although it can be controlled by cutting back. The leaves vary in shape and size from fine tapering, ribbon shapes up to 4 in (10 cm) long and $\frac{1}{3}$ in (8 mm) wide with blunt ends, to broad, shiny, spoon-shaped leathery leaves, 3 in (8 cm) long and up to 3 in (8 cm) wide. The beautiful azure-blue flowers, with purple centres and yellow blotches, are produced on erect stems.

*E. crassipes* (water hyacinth) The mid-green, smooth and ladle-shaped leaves grow in floating rosettes. Each

leaf stalk is swollen and contains spongy tissue, which keeps the plant afloat. The very decorative, blue-black, feathery roots provide a refuge for small fish and a support for fish eggs. The eye-catching flowers are produced in the centre of the rosettes on a spike that is about 6 in (15 cm) tall and that holds as many as 10–30 individual flowers. Each pale mauvish flower has a very definite 'eye' marking of gold and blue. In warm waters it is notorious for spreading prolifically by means of stolons and has choked many temperate-zone waterways.

## Eleocharis

The 200 or so species are found in most parts of the world. They vary greatly in size, but all grow rhizomatously and are propagated by runner cuttings or from nutlets formed on the rhizome. Although adaptable to many growing conditions, they do best with no more than 4 in (10 cm) of water over their crowns.

*E. acicularis* (hair grass) The very fine, pale green, rush-like leaves, 2–12 in (5–30 cm) long according to the depth of the water, grow in little bunches. It is a good transition plant for marrying the pool edge to the rest of the landscape, as it will grow submerged or in damp soil. It is a native to America, Europe, Asia and Australia.

*E. dulcis* (*E. tuberosa*) (Chinese water chestnut) A native to eastern Asia, the Pacific islands and west Africa, it is much grown because of its crisp-textured tubers, 2 in (5 cm) thick, which are eaten raw or cooked. The plant has clumps of fresh green, narrow, spike-like stems, 1–3 ft (30–90 cm) tall, occasionally terminating in 2 in (5 cm) flower spikelets. Apart from its use in food production, it is an elegant shallow-water, vertical-accent plant. As it enters winter dormancy it exhibits beautiful autumn colours.

## Euryale ferox (Gorgon plant)

The common name is derived from the plant's thorny appearance, which seemed to recall the fierce thorny locks of the mythological Gorgon. Introduced into Europe in 1809 by the Director of the Calcutta Botanic Gardens, William Roxburgh, it was believed to be the largest aquatic in existence until the discovery of the Victoria (see below). It is a native to southeast Asia and China, where it was cultivated for centuries as a food plant. It has flat, spiny leaves 4–5 ft (1.2–1.5 m) across, which have prominent veins on the purple undersides.

Opposite above: *Eichornia crassipes* (water hyacinth); opposite below: *Euryale ferox* (gorgon plant)

The upper surfaces are olive-green with a puckered spiny surface, which, unlike that of the Victoria, does not turn up at the edges. The leaves are not long-lived but are quickly replaced. The small violet-blue flowers, which are about 2 in (5 cm) long and short-lived, are barely held above the water. It is treated as an annual and requires only a little more warmth than the hardy waterlilies. It requires a good-sized planting crate, at least 8 in (20 cm) deep and 20 in (50 cm) in diameter.

## Hydrilla verticillata

A submerged water weed, the importation or sale of this plant has been banned in the United States. Its aggressive habit in temperate locations has caused it to interfere with navigation of waterways, hinder fishery production, clog drainage systems and choke out other, more desirable aquatic plants. It is native to central Europe, Asia and Australia. Similar to the more common Elodea, it has a reddish midrib, and the leaf margins are toothed whereas in Elodea they are smooth. The stems are 6–12 in (15–30 cm) long, forming many branches. The narrow leaves, which are in rosettes, are $\frac{3}{4}$ in (19 mm) long and very slender. It is all too easily propagated by cuttings.

## Hydrocleys nymphoides (Limnocharis humboldtii) (water poppy)

Found in Central America and south to Argentina, this plant has shiny, sap-green, floating leaves, 2 in (5 cm) across. They are broadly heart-shaped or circular, similar to those of a waterlily, and borne on long trailing stems. There is a spongy tissue present in the leaves, which help them to float. The beautiful but short-lived, shiny-yellow flowers, which are constantly being replaced, are 2–2$\frac{1}{2}$ in (5–6 cm) in diameter, and are composed of three petals with a brown centre. The root is a rhizome, which encourages the plant to spread rapidly. It grows best in water about 12 in (30 cm) deep with plenty of light, and although it may grow outdoors in the summer it must be wintered indoors where winters are harsh. Grown in tubs with a loam base, it makes a good partner in pools with tropical waterlilies and lotus. It is propagated by division and by cuttings.

## Hygrophila

A genus of tropical herbs adapting to aquatic conditions mainly from southern Asia and Africa. All listed grow best with no more than 2 in (5 cm) of water over their crowns. All are tender to frost.

*H. angustifolia* (*H. salicifolia*) (willow leaf hygrophila) A native from southern China to Sri Lanka and also Australia and New Zealand, it reaches 30–40 in (76–100 cm) in height. The plant has thin leaves, 4–8 in

*Hydrocleys nymphoides* (water poppy)

(10–20 cm) long and only $\frac{1}{4}$–$\frac{1}{2}$ in (6–12 mm) wide. The leaf blade passes gently over into a short leaf stalk and is often arched upwards. The young leaves are reddish and covered with a fine down, while the older leaves, which resemble willow foliage, are a pale green. Under bright light the colour of the leaves may change to brown. The central vein on the upper surface is reddish. The stems are slightly square. If too warm, over 77°F (25°C), the internodes become elongated and the plant is too straggly for decoration. It is best planted on its own rather than in groups. The very small flowers are bright purple, almost violet, in dense clusters in the leaf axils. It can be grown out of the water, when the aerial leaves take on an arched shape.

*H. difformis (Synnema triflora)* (water wistaria) A native to southeast Asia, it is fast growing, quickly achieving a height of 12–16 in (30–41 cm). The attractive, stalkless leaves are oval and dark green, similar to those of the wholly hardy Houttuynia. Good light is essential. The water temperature also greatly affects the plants' appearance, and the leaves will remain quite dwarf if the temperature is lower than 75°F (24°C). The mauve flowers are produced in clusters in the axils of the leaves.

*H. polysperma* (dwarf hygrophila) Originating from Bangladesh to Thailand, this plant forms attractive green tufts, which grow to the surface in good light. It is tolerant of temperatures ranging from 61° to 86°F (16–30°C), and it is suitable for shallow outdoor pools in the summer. The stems, many of which are laterally branched, will grow to a height of 20 in (50 cm), producing a dense appearance. The sparse, soft-green leaves are slightly hairy and egg-shaped, 2 in (5 cm) long and $\frac{1}{2}$ in (12 mm) wide, with brownish tinges. The aerial leaves are narrower and darker green. The flowers, which are rarely seen, appear above the water.

### Hymenocallis liriosme (spider lily)

Growing up to 2 ft (61 cm) in height, this bulbous aquatic plant grows with up to 6 in (15 cm) of water over its crown. It boasts large, spider-like, fragrant, white blossoms in late summer. The long, strap-like leaves, which are green, are winter-dormant and will survive outdoors where the soil does not freeze.

### Ipomoea aquatica (water spinach, aquatic morning glory)

This shallow-water, vining plant is native to Asia, Taiwan and southern China, yet it has a much wider distribution throughout all tropical regions of the world. Commercially, it is cultivated extensively in

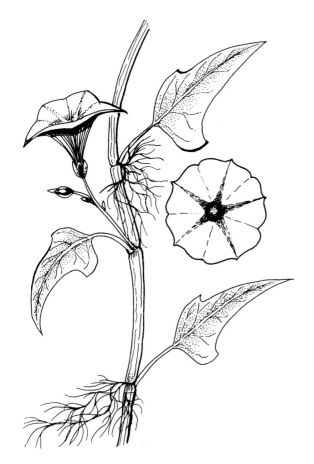

*Ipomoea aquatica*

China and the Far East, where young leaves and stems are boiled or fried as a vegetable dish. In some countries the plant is used as livestock fodder; elsewhere it is used medicinally in the treatment of intestinal disorders caused by contaminated water. The plant is extremely aggressive in warm, frost-free areas, spreading by running stems, which root where they touch soil. The leaves of the plant are medium green and oval or arrow-shaped, 2–6 in (5–15 cm) long. The flowers are the classic, funnel-shaped, morning-glory type, $1\frac{1}{4}$ in (3 cm) in diameter, pink to purplish in colour, with a purple centre. Bloom quantity and frequency are dependent on light intensity. The plant grows best in very wet soil or in water up to 3 in (7 cm) deep. Propagation is by division or by cutting. Sales and shipping of *I. aquatica* are restricted in the United States.

## Jussiaea (water primrose)

Similar to Ludwigia (see below), these surface creepers bear striking, bright yellow flowers resembling butter-cups up to 2 in (5 cm) in diameter. They are best rooted in soil below 6–12 in (15–31 cm) of water. They are suitable for tub gardens or frost-free pools in the sun.

*J. longifolia* (primrose willow) With glaucous green, willow-like leaves, this plant will stand erect 2–3 ft (0.6–0.9 m) above the water.

*J. repens* (*Ludwigia adscendens*) (primrose creeper) Rapid growth and glossy green, oval leaves, 1 in (2 cm) long, distinguish this plant, which may be invasive.

## Limnobium stolonifera (L. laevigatum) (Amazonian frogbit)

A near relative of the hardier frogbit, *Hydrocharis morsus-ranae*, this is a floating aquatic from Mexico and Brazil. It has thick swollen leaves, $\frac{1}{2}-\frac{3}{4}$ in (1–2 cm) in diameter, containing spongy tissue for buoyancy. The leaf blades are heart- /or egg-shaped on very short leaf stalks. Male and female flowers are produced on separate plants, the female flowers being greenish-white and arranged in threes. It is capable of growing outside in a pool provided it is brought in for winter protection. The best winter treatment is to allow it to root in mud and to keep it light and warm and surrounded by moist air. There is a larger species, *L. spongia* (American frogbit), which has both sexes of flower on the same plant. Propagated by division, they thrive best if they receive 12 hours of good light each day.

## Limnocharis flava

A handsome tropical swamp plant, which grows to 1–2 ft (30–60 cm) and which can be grown in tubs or summer pools. The long-stalked flowers, which are yellow with a white border, are $\frac{3}{4}-1\frac{1}{2}$ in (2–4 cm) across and produced in July. The spear-like leaves are blunt-ended, about 1–2 in (2–5 cm) long and sheathed at the base. It requires a temperature of 65°F (18°C). It has a stoloniferous habit and is easily propagated by division.

## Ludwigia

There are about 20 species of aquatic Ludwigia with widespread distribution. Any flowers are small and inconspicuous. The aquatic species flourish in warmer countries, where they grow completely submerged in pool margins. The leaves are mainly smooth, simple and alternate, $2-4\frac{1}{2}$ in (5–12 cm) long.

*L. mullertii* (*L. natans, L. repens*) (swamp spoon, red ludwigia) This is the most commonly grown species from tropical South America that is suitable for summer pools. It has glossy, olive-green leaves above with reddish undersides. The slender stems bear small yellow flowers in the leaf axils. It is a very good submerged oxygenator and tips the water surface with creeping runners.

117

*Marsilea quadrifolia*

### Marsilea quadrifolia (water clover)

A genus of amphibious and aquatic ferns resembling four-leaved clovers, which have a worldwide distribution mainly from tropical and sub-tropical areas. It is largely grown in tropical pools, where the attractive floating or erect leaves are borne on long slender stalks and creeping rhizomes. There are two similar species – *M. drummondii*, the water clover from western Australia, which has fan-like leaflets 3 in (8 cm) in diameter and whitish hairs and wavy margins, and *M. quadrifolia*, from Europe and Asia, with slightly smaller leaflets, 1 in (2 cm) across, which are not hairy, and rounded margins.

### Myriophyllum aquaticum (M. brasiliense, M. proserpinacoides) (parrot's feather)

A native to Brazil and Argentina, this is a rambling amphibious plant. It is useful for oxygenating and can be allowed to climb out of the water to form an elegant cover for any hard or ugly sides of the pool. The spirally arranged leaves, which grow in dense whorls around the stems, are delicately feathery and whitish-green in colour. The shoots can grow to enormous lengths from small cuttings in no time, either lying on the surface of the water or at the pool edge where they will droop over the edge of a pool, turning up at the ends. Cuttings are easily overwintered in frost-free water or mud.

### Nymphoides (Limnanthemum) (floating heart)

These plants from mainly tropical and sub-tropical regions are similar in habit to waterlilies. They have round to heart-shaped floating leaves and delicate flowers held above the water. They are particularly attractive in shallow water where they grow readily in rich loam. Take care not to let them get out of hand.

*N. aquatica* (banana plant, fairy waterlily) This species from southeast North America has white flowers $\frac{3}{4}$ in (19 mm) across, which are held above round green leaves with purple spots, 6 in (15 cm) across. The roots form runners with erect shoots and swollen, adventitious roots resembling tiny bunches of bananas.

*N. germanica* Bright yellow, feathery flowers crown the mat of chocolate brown leaves patterned with green leaves formed by this species. The plant will thrive with 6–10 in (15–25 cm) of water over its crown, and it spreads by sending out rhizomatous runners.

*N. humboldtiana* This species from tropical America has fringed white flowers with yellow centres and dark green, kidney-shaped leaves, 6 in (15 cm) across.

*N. indica* (water snowflake) This species will grow in 3 ft (0.9 m) of water, supporting small, round leaves, 2–8 in (5–20 cm) across, with a heart-shaped base. The short-lived, freely produced dainty flowers are white, yellowish in the middle, and sometimes produced in the axils of floating leaves.

### Pistia stratiotes (water lettuce)
A beautiful floating plant, originally from tropical America, which has rosettes of leaves, soft green and velvety, 4–6 in (10–15 cm) long, and extensive hanging roots. Well-grown specimen plants in cultivation are capable of growing to 12 in (30 cm) in diameter. Like the water hyacinth (*Eichhornia crassipes*), the plant is capable of colonizing large expanses of lakes and rivers. It has become naturalized in many tropical areas. Propagation is normally from the stolons, which are liberally produced, but young seedlings resembling duckweed can result from the flowers hidden inconspicuously between the leaves. The extensive network of young white roots, which turn black as they mature, is a good refuge for fish eggs and fry.

### Proserpinaca palustris (mermaid weed)
This native to the southern United States spreads by means of branched, creeping stems that, when rooted in soil at the pool bottom, can grow through at least 2 ft

*Nymphoides* (floating heart)

(61 cm) of water to the pool's surface. The submerged green leaves, which are 1–1¾ in (2–4.5 cm) long, are deeply divided and feathery. As the plant emerges to form a mat-like water cover, the leaves become lance shaped, with serrated margins, and 1½–2¾ in (4–7 cm) long. The flowers are insignificant, and the plant is grown chiefly for its interesting foliage and to control the growth of algae by blocking sunlight to the pool surface. Propagation is by division or seed.

### Rotala rotundifolia
A lovely, creeping, shallow-water plant. It is widespread in southeast Asia, where it grows either in muddy habitats or as a marginal in water. It has small round leaves, ½ in (12 mm) in diameter and arranged in whorls, which are dark green. It will tolerate fairly cool water but prefers temperatures around 68°F (20°C). It grows best with its roots in soil 2–6 in (5–15 cm) below the water's surface and in good light.

### Sagittaria (arrowheads)
This genus has worldwide distribution, although most come from America. There are both hardy and tropical forms, and they exhibit a great variety of leaf-shapes, from the young, strap-like submerged leaves to the

Above and below: *Pistia stratiotes* (water lettuce)

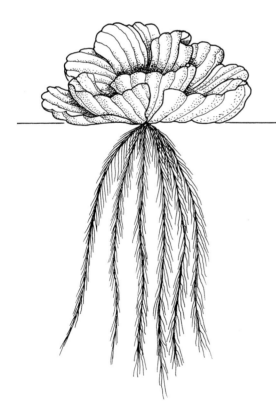

longer floating leaves and the distinctive arrow-shaped leaves, which are held above the water and give the plant its common name. Runners produce edible tubers.

*S. lancifolia ruminoides* (red-stemmed sagittaria) The distinctive features of this sub-tropical plant are its striking red stems which hold bold green leaves 4 ft (1.2 m) above the water's surface. White flowers are borne on stalks in summer. It grows best in good sun and with up to 6 in (15 cm) of water over its crown.

*S. montevidensis* One of the more dramatic and handsome species available for warm water, it can grow up to 6 ft (2 m), with each leaf 1–2 ft (0.6–0.9 m) long. The large flowers are white, and each petal is blotched with purple at the base.

### Salvinia auriculata
A small floating fern from tropical America and Africa, which has become acclimatized to some temperate areas. The oval leaves are $1\frac{1}{2}$ in (4 cm) long, a pale green colour and hairy on the surface. It has tiny, trailing roots. It flourishes in warm pools associated with tropical waterlilies and water hyacinths.

### Scirpus cernuus (Isolepis gracilis) (low bulrush)
This graceful, brilliant green moisture-lover has arch-

ing, thread-like stems, topped by small brown flower spikelets. It grows up to 10 in (25 cm) high in moderate to bright light. It can be grown as an indoor pot plant or in water up to 2 in (5 cm) over its crown. It makes an elegant pool-edge plant in temperate conditions.

## Thalia dealbata

A native of southern North America, this tall marginal aquatic plant, about 5 ft (1.5 m) tall, has spreading panicles of violet flowers held nearly 10 ft (3 m) high and leaves that are glaucous blue and canna-like, dusted with white powder. It will also grow out of the water in marshy situations. It has thick leaves, 20 in (50 cm) long and 10 in (25 cm) wide, borne on long leaf stalks. It can be grown outside during the summer in temperate climates and lifted from the pool for frost protection during the winter. It is a fine architectural plant, suitable as a specimen plant in both formal and informal settings. There is a red-stemmed species, *T. geniculata rubra*.

## Trapa natans (water chestnut)

An aquatic annual with floating leaves that is becoming rarer in its native southern Europe but that has become naturalized in Australia and North America. The thorny fruits, which are often eaten, are large, black woody nuts, which should be collected in the autumn and stored in cool water for the winter. As they bear four projections, they resemble the shape of the caltrop, a four-spiked iron ball thrown to maim cavalry horses, and it is also known as the water caltrop. On germinating, the single-seeded fruit bears a long stalk capable of growing in a wide variety of water depths. These long stalks bear the attractive rosettes of mottled leaves that are up to 20 in (50 cm) across. Spongy tissue inside the leaf stalks enables them to float, and the triangular leaf blades are toothed on the front margin. The flowers, which appear in late summer, are small and insignificant. The plant has become an invasive nuisance in some waterways, and its sale is restricted in the United States.

## Vallisneria spiralis (tape grass)

A favourite submerged plant for the aquarium because of its tolerance of a wide range of conditions, this plant is also used as an oxygenator in temperate pools. It is native to tropical and sub-tropical zones of both hemispheres. The light green, ribbon-like leaves are distinguished by serrations on the tips of their leaves. If the water depth is inadequate, the leaves bend to a horizontal position at the water's surface. Pollination requires the less common male flowers, which are borne on separate plants, to release pollen on the surface of the water. The female flowers, which are borne on spirally

*Thalia dealbata*

twisting stems, rise to the surface and float until pollinated. The most commonly grown species of Vallisneria is *V. spiralis*, which has leaves up to 32 in (80 cm) long, and $\frac{1}{6}-\frac{1}{3}$ in (4–8 mm) wide. The word *spiralis* refers to the twisted flower stalk and not, as is widely thought, the leaves. There is a form of *V. spiralis* called *tortifolia*; that is slightly shorter and it has wider leaves, which are twisted along their entire length. *V. americana* and *V. gigantea* are much larger plants and require very much deeper water. The leaves of *V. gigantea* can grow to 6 ft (1.8 m) long.

## Victoria amazonica (giant waterlily, Amazonian waterlily)

This amazing plant was discovered in South America in 1801. The first seeds were not, however, sent to England until 1837, and from then the major horticultural institutions rivalled each other to achieve a flower of the new plant. Sir Joseph Paxton, head gardener to the 6th Duke of Devonshire at Chatsworth in Derbyshire, succeeded in flowering the plant in the giant conservatory on the estate.

The huge circular leaves, which grow to 6–7 ft (1.8–2.1 m) in diameter, have a most beautiful network of veins on the underside, and some people believe that this venation inspired Paxton in his design of the ill-fated Crystal Palace, a huge conservatory, which was rebuilt in Sydenham, northwest of London, after being dismantled from the Great Exhibition in Hyde Park in 1851. The Crystal Palace was destroyed by fire in 1936, and the conservatory at Chatsworth suffered a similar tragic end when the 9th Duke blew up the building in 1919 after many of the plants had died as a result of fuel shortage.

The generic name Victoria commemorates Queen Victoria, who was presented with a leaf and a flower of the newly imported wonder in 1849.

The flowers and leaves emerge from a thick rhizome, about 8 in (20 cm) in diameter. The young leaves, which are about 6 in (15 cm) in diameter, are crumpled but soon take the form of small circular tea-trays about 12 in (30 cm) across. Depending on the depth and warmth of the water and the day length and intensity of light, growth is very rapid, and in two or three weeks the leaves assume a diameter of 6–7 ft (1.8–2.1 m). Shallow water tends to reduce the length of the leafstalk and consequent leaf size.

The leaves are a fresh green colour, and the upturned red edges, 2–8 in (5–20 cm) high, give rise to one of the common native names, water platter. Rain from severe storms drains off the leaves through a depression near the leaf stalks and through minute pores on the surface of the leaves. The upper leaf surface exhibits numerous low mounds, which trap air in a honeycomb of interlocking air pockets between the ribs on the underside of the leaf. This gives the leaf great buoyancy, which can be sufficient to support great weights. (Although Victorias have been frequently photographed with children sitting on the leaves, a closer examination of the pictures will often reveal a floating support under the leaf designed to distribute the weight evenly over the whole surface.) The purplish undersides of the leaves are dramatic, with massive veins and ribs radiating from the centre and projecting into the water in a skeletal fashion.

The nocturnal flowers are equally impressive. They start life as prickly pear-shaped flower buds, up to 8 in (20 cm) across. The mature flowers have numerous white petals (80 have been counted) and can reach 12–14 in (30–36 cm) across on opening. The colour later changes to pink, then purplish-red on successive evenings. Robert Schomburgk, whose expedition was responsible for the first viable seeds being sent to Britain in 1837, recalled how, as the amazing flowers opened in the dusk, they released an intoxicating fragrance similar to that of crushed pineapple. Each flower lasts for three days, closing shortly after sunrise on the third morning in a glowing purplish colour and sinking under the water where it rots and later distributes the large, shiny seed pods containing the pea-like seeds. Self-pollination occurs as the flower opens and closes during its three-day cycle, trapping aquatic beetles and insects, which transfer the pollen.

There is some dispute whether the Victoria is annual or perennial, but it is normally cultivated as an annual, thus allowing the compost in the large root container required for its growth to be replaced every season. After collection the seed is stored in distilled water at a minimum temperature of 65°F (18°C) and sown in January or February at 85°F (29°C). The seed is filed to break through the tough seed coat and sown in pans of loam and sand about 1 in (2 cm) under the water in a heated aquarium.

After germination the first leaf is grass-like; the second is arrow-headed; and later leaves assume the normal circular outline, although initially without the upturned edge. The seedling is potted as soon as possible into a 3½ in (9 cm) pot of loam and sand. As the first true adult leaves develop, a larger container, about 12 in (30 cm) in diameter and 8 in (20 cm) deep, should be used. A lining material will facilitate the easy removal of young plant and compost to the permanent planting position. The water temperature is kept at 85°F (29°C) until the plant is better established, and 2–3 in (5–8 cm) of water should cover the container. During this critical period in the plant's growth, air temperatures are kept ideally at 75°F (24°C) in the day and at 65°F (18°C) at night.

The final planting position requires a pool with a minimum diameter of 25 ft (7.6 m) and a planting receptacle for the roots that is 6 ft (1.8 m) in diameter and 2 ft (60 cm) deep. The compost should be fibrous rich loam as specified for waterlilies (see page 30). The top of the container should be 15–18 in (38–46 cm) below the water surface. Final planting takes place in March or April, when the leaves are around 6–7 in (15–18 cm) in diameter.

After final planting the water temperature can be allowed to settle between 75° and 80°F (24°–27°C) and a minimum night air temperature of 65°F (18°C). Throughout the growing season the plant should be given maximum light and frequent feeding. Compound organic fertilizers are mixed with water to form golf ball-sized pellets, and these are inserted and covered in the compost every two weeks. Flowering normally begins in May and growth tails off during October. Throughout the growing season spent foliage and blossoms should be removed. Growth and bloom period can be extended by supplementary lighting.

One other species and one variety are grown. *V. cruziana (trikeri)*, the Santa Cruz waterlily, is found in more southerly locations than the Amazonian species and is more often seen in cultivation. The flowers are similar but earlier, and the leaves are a lighter green. The underside of the leaf is a darker red. It is reputed to be slightly hardier. *V.* 'Longwood Hybrid', which was raised at Longwood Gardens, Pennsylvania, is a hybrid between *V. amazonia* and *V. cruziana*.

### Wachendorfia thrysiflora
This native to South Africa bears deeply grooved, sabre-like, medium green foliage, up to 3 ft (91 cm) long.

Dramatic, 6 ft (1.8 m) stems bear spires of yellow, funnel-like flowers, each 3 in (8 cm) long. The plant grows best in very damp soil (although it will adapt to 4 in (10 cm) of water over the crown) and in full sun. Propagation is by division or by seed.

## Xanthosoma

These attractive marginal aroid plants from tropical America have arrow-shaped leaves resembling those of the Colocasias (taros). The rootstocks are rich in starch, and the cultivated forms bear only a few large leaves at the top of the plant. Two species only, *X. lindenii* and *X. violaceum*, are worthy of planting as pool specimens, and these plants will thrive best with 2–6 in (5–15 cm) of water over their crowns.

*X. lindenii* A striking variegated form from Colombia. It has tuberous roots and is often used as a house plant if it can be grown with ample water. The glossy green leaves, 18 in (46 cm) long, have white veins and midribs and are borne on long leaf stalks, which are longer than

Above: The huge leaves of the Victoria and, below, one of the nocturnal, short-lived flowers

the leaf blades. The white, arum-like flowers are 6 in (15 cm) long. The plants can grow to 2 ft 6 in (76 cm) tall.

*X. violaceum* (blue taro) Native to the West Indies, this species has purple leaf stalks, 2 ft 6 in (76 cm) long, and purple margins on leaves measuring up to 2 ft (0.6 m) long and 18 in (46 cm) wide. It is an attractive specimen plant for the edge of tropical pools. The tubers are edible but have to be boiled first to destroy their acrid properties. The flowers are yellow and arum-like and 12 in (30 cm) long.

## Zantedeschia
In its native habitat of South Africa, this plant is often found inhabiting drainage ditches and swampy areas. The common, native name, pig lily, conveys the low esteem with which it is regarded. However, where it is not so easily cultivated, the undeniable beauty of its classic form is highly appreciated.

*Zantedeschia aethiopica* (calla or arum lily)

*Z. aethiopica* (calla lily, arum lily) A South African species with blooms well known as cut flowers. Although sometimes classed as hardy in England, it is resistant to frost only when its crown is submerged in 9 in (23 cm) of water. The leaves, which are borne on fleshy stalks, are glossy and arrow-shaped, nearly 12 in (30 cm) long and 6 in (15 cm) wide. The pure white flowers contain deep golden pokers, 5–6 in (12–15 cm) long, and they appear profusely throughout the summer.

*Z.a.* 'Green Goddess' A modern hybrid of the species, 'Green Goddess' is a striking plant whose leaves and flowers are prized by florists. The glossy, deep green leaves have ruffled margins. The white flower bracts, which are streaked with the same green, encircle a bright yellow central spike. The tips of both the leaves and of the flowers are somewhat elongated, and the effect of the entire plant in a pool setting is quite dramatic. 'Green Goddess' is only slightly more tender than the species.

# HARDY AQUATICS

## Acorus

A group of aromatic perennials with iris-like leaves, related to Zantedeschia. The name derives from the Greek word *kore* (a pupil), which refers to the plants' use in opthalmy, and the genus has had a reputation as a medicinal herb for thousands of years. Most commonly grown are the *Calamus* species, the sweet flags, whose common name arises from all parts of the plant having a sweet scent, especially when crushed or bruised, which was used in medieval times to mask musty odours.

*A. calamus* (sweet flag, sweet sedge)
A native to eastern Asia but now naturalized in Europe and North America, this was probably introduced into Europe in the 16th century. It was used as a floor covering before the days of carpets, particularly in churches and castles and on special occasions. Growing on river banks and at the edge of streams and canals in shallow water and full sun, *A. calamus* has green, iris-like leaves, up to 2 ft 6 in (76 cm) tall, which, when crushed, give off a strong tangerine-like scent. The insignificant brownish-green flowers are 2–3 in (5–8 cm) long, borne in densely packed, arum-like spikes, and grow towards the top of the stems. It grows best with 3–5 in (8–13 cm) of water over its crown. In North America the flowers are successful in producing red-berried fruits, but it does not fruit in Britain where it relies upon the spreading rhizome for its main propagation. The rhizome produces an oil used in perfumery and, in North America, a sweetbread.

*A. calamus variegatus* (variegated sweet flag) This variegated form of *A. calamus* has green and creamy-white striped aromatic leaves. The flowers are insignificant brownish green spikes, 2–3 in (5–8 cm) long, which grow close together towards the tops of the stems. This is a very attractive, slower growing, and more compact plant than *A. calamus*. It is propagated by division in spring and is grown in the same way as *A. calamus*.

*A. gramineus* (Japanese rush) A native to China and Japan, this is an attractive, dwarf, clump-forming, slender-leaved plant, ideal for the small pool or tub garden. The almost grass-like dark green leaves, which tend to grow at a slight angle from the root, are evergreen and resemble a dwarf iris. It is easily propagated by division in spring, growing to 1 ft (31 cm) tall and thriving with up to 4 in (10 cm) of water over its crown.

*A. gramineus variegatus* (variegated Japanese rush) A slender-leaved variegated plant with green and cream stripes running down the leaf. The plant grows in close tufts to about 10 in (25 cm) tall, making it particularly attractive and ideally suited to a small pool or tub. The variegation is so attractive that it is also grown as a houseplant. Propagation is by division in spring, and culture is as for *A. gramineus*.

## Alisma

These shallow-water plants have plantain-like leaves and bear small white or rosy-coloured flowers throughout the season. They are notorious for spreading rapidly by self-seeding, so old flower heads should be removed as soon as flowering is over. The roots were once used as a powerful sedative, and cattle have been known to be harmed when digesting the acrid sap.

*A. gramineum (arcuatum)* A species from North America that grows either as a marginal or as a submerged plant. The aerial leaves are spoon-shaped and 20 in (50 cm) long, whereas the submerged leaves are strap-shaped. The pinkish-white flowers are 12 in (30 cm) high.

*A. plantago-aquatica* (water plantain) Once known as the 'mad dog weed' and native to northern temperate regions, the plant has medium-green leaves, which are slightly heart-shaped with distinct veining on long stalks. The eye-catching pyramid-shaped flower head is about 3 ft (90 cm) high and bears an abundance of three-petalled rosy-lilac flowers. Remove spent flower heads if seeding becomes a problem. Propagation is by seed in spring or by division. The plant will grow with up to 6 in (15 cm) of water over its crown.

*A. parviflora* This attractive plant from North America bears pyramidal panicles of small pink or white flowers, which rise above the rounded foliage. It is quick to establish itself in the pool. During the winter the leaves fall into the water and become skeletonized. Propagation is by division of established plants or by seed sown in shallow pans just covered by water in spring. This plant, which grows up to 18 in (46 cm) tall, thrives with 0.5 in (0.13 cm) of water over its crown.

## Aponogeton distachyus (water hawthorn, Cape pondweed)

Native to South Africa, this is a most desirable plant for all pools. The beautiful, heavily-scented, waxy flowers consist of two opposed spikes on long flower stalks, the origin of the specific name *distachyus*. The stalks are 2–3 in (5–8 cm) long, and each spike bears large alternate white bracts, at the base of which the flowers are arranged in a double row. The flowers, highlighted by jet-black anthers, are produced freely in two main flowering times – early summer and autumn, even into the winter in mild conditions. The white flowers gradually turn green as they age, bending back into the water where the fruit ripens. When mature, the fruits rise to the surface and distribute the seeds, which float away to ensure good dispersal. They soon sink to the bottom and germinate if the water is not too deep. If the seed is harvested, it should be sown while fresh on to a compost of loam and sand, 2–3 in (5–8 cm) deep, in a watertight container and covered by 4 in (10 cm) of water. The water temperature should be 55–60°F (13–15°C) for germination to take place.

The floating mature leaves are borne on long leaf stalks and are strap-shaped, with leaf blades 10 in (25 cm) long. This shape is perfectly adapted to slight movements of the water. The roots consist of walnut-sized tubers, which should be planted in heavy loam in large waterlily containers. They should be planted initially in water no deeper than 6 in (15 cm) and later, if required, moved to water as deep as 2 ft (61 cm). It is said that in South Africa the flowers and flower stems are used as a flavouring in a meat stew. The tubers are also edible. This plant will bloom all winter in temperate zones and will tolerate some shade.

## Azolla caroliniana (fairy moss)

A native to sub-tropical America, this delicate little floating plant has acclimatized itself to Britain. It is a small fern with attractive floating fronds, $\frac{1}{3}$ in (8 mm) in diameter, which are pale green with fine hair-like roots on the undersides. As winter approaches, the fronds become tinted with red, crimson and brown before disintegrating and producing overwintering bodies. As a precaution, keep a few plants indoors, either on saturated pans of compost or in shallow pans of water, in good light and in a frost-free place. It does not make a good aquarium subject because of its need for high light levels. Although it is capable of spreading rapidly and completely covering the surface of a small pool, it does help to reduce algae growth in the initial establishment of a new pond. In small areas it can be easily netted off if it becomes a nuisance. It is not suggested for introduction into large pools or lakes where it may become a problem.

## Butomus umbellatus (flowering rush)

A native to Europe, including Britain, this is a very striking plant that grows along the margins of streams, lakes and wet marshlands. It has long, rich green leaves, $\frac{1}{3}$ in (8 mm) wide, triangular in section tapering to a point at their tips and often reaching 3 ft (90 cm) in height. The leaves are bronzy-purple when young and sheathed at the base. The edges of the leaves are so sharp that they can cut the mouths of grazing animals, a characteristic that gave rise to the generic name – *bous* (an ox), *temmo* (to cut). The flowering stalks are even taller. They have umbels of up to 30 beautiful, three-petalled, dainty pink flowers. It is propagated by division or by removing the tiny bulbils that grow along the length of the rootstock and planting them in wet mud until they are large enough to be introduced at the sides of the permanent pool. It will grow with 3–5 in (8–13 cm) of water over its crown.

## Calla palustris (bog arum)

A native to Europe, north Asia and North America, this marginal plant should not be confused with Zantedeschia, which is sometimes called the calla lily and which is rather similar although larger. The true calla plant produces a neat clump of beautiful dark green, shiny, cordate leaves, about 8–12 in (20–30 cm) long, borne on a long creeping rhizome. The rambling spread of the rhizome and the dense cluster of foliage, make it an ideal plant to scramble over the edge of a pool between water and mud. In early summer the plants are covered with small white papery, arum-like flowers with orange spike-like centres. If pollinated, which is often undertaken by water snails, the flowers turn into stout red spikes of striking red berries in the autumn. It prefers still water, 0–4 in (0–10 cm) over its crown. Propagation is by breaking off pieces of rootstock in spring and inserting these into the wet soil by the water's edge. Laplanders are reported to boil the bitter rhizomes and to make them into a sort of bread.

## Callitriche autumnalis (*hermaphroditica*) (water starwort)

A submerged cold-water oxygenating plant native to most regions. The generic name, meaning 'beautiful hair', refers to the foliage. The long, thin branching stems support small, light green linear leaves, $\frac{2}{3}-\frac{3}{4}$ in (1–2 cm) long, which become crowded in dense rosettes near the surface. There are also aerial lance-like leaves. In addition to its oxygenating value, it is an unusual plant for the fishkeeper, for the tangled growth holds spawn well and fish eat the young growth. It is a fast-

Opposite above: Azolla caroliniana (fairy moss); opposite below: *Butomus umbellatus* (flowering rush)

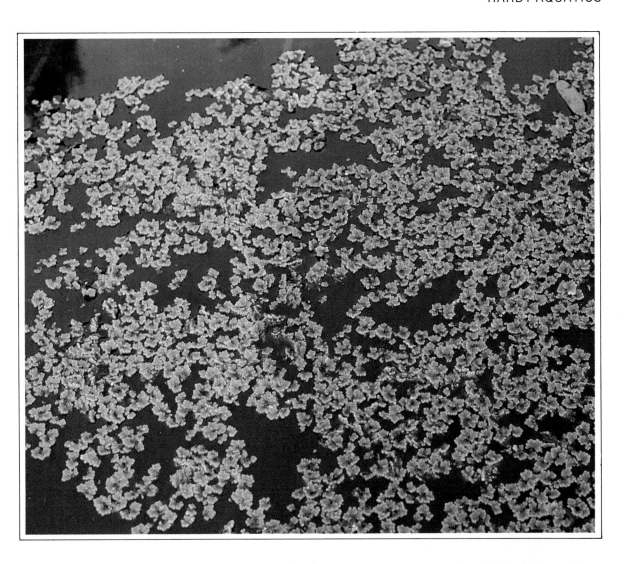

*Caltha palustris* (marsh marigold)

growing plant and has the additional bonus of continuing to grow throughout the winter months. There is a form, *C. platycarpa (verna)*, which is at its best in spring and dies down in the winter. It is distinguished from *C. autumnalis* by the presence of small, star-like hairs all over the plant. The flowers are insignificant. It is propagated by division or by cuttings.

### Caltha palustris (marsh marigold, king cup)

This native to Europe and North America is a beautiful marginal aquatic plant, which enjoys being in or near shallow water up to 3 in (8 cm) deep. It is a good plant for pool margins that are wet in spring but likely to dry out in mid- to late summer, when the plant starts to lose its foliage. It starts to flower in March and continues until May, bearing clusters of cup-shaped, yellow, buttercup-like flowers. The generic name owes its origin to the Greek word *kalathos*, a goblet. The heart-shaped or kidney-shaped leaves are 2–3 in (5–8 cm) across in the spring, growing to 12 in (30 cm) in the summer. They are dark green and shiny, and the whole plant quickly forms bold tufts of dark green with stout branching stems. Highly recommended as one of the best marginal plants, it should be grown in groups rather than as single specimens. Propagation is by root

Opposite: *Calla palustris* (bog arum)

division or from fresh seed sown in spring. Old herbalists claimed that the plant is a good cure for anaemia and epilepsy, although Frances Perry unearthed a reference claiming that the flowers should never be taken into a girl's room 'lest she be liable to fits of madness'. Although the plant is reputed to be poisonous to livestock, the leaves have been regularly used as 'spring greens' in New England. It is somewhat prone to mildew, but this does not seriously affect the plant's beauty.

*C. palustris* 'Alba' (white marsh marigold) This extremely attractive variety from the Himalayas produces small white flowers with bright yellow centres. The rounded leaves, 6–9 in (15–23 cm) tall, have a finely serrated edge. Propagation is by root division or by seed.

*C. palustris flore plena* (double marsh marigold; sometimes called 'Monstrosa' in the U.S.) A really beautiful plant, which produces so many double flowers that the hummock of leaves, 9 in (23 cm) across, is almost hidden. An added bonus to this variety is that it often flowers twice in one year. Propagation is by root division. Cultivation is as for *C. palustris*.

*C. polypetala* (giant marsh marigold) A native to Asia Minor, this plant produces an abundance of attractive, 3 ft (0.9 m) tall, single-yellow flowers, which rise above very large, dark green leaves, 10–12 in (25–30 cm) in diameter. It is a truly magnificent plant for the larger pool. Propagation is by root division or by seed. It will thrive with 0–5 in (0–13 cm) of water over its crown.

## Ceratophyllum demersum (hornwort, coon tails)
A submerged aquatic, which has almost worldwide distribution, this is suitable as an oxygenating plant in outdoor pools or aquaria because it is better able to flourish in warm water than many other of the hardy oxygenating plants. In favourable conditions it may reach nearly 6 ft (1.8 m) in length and may take the form of large floating clumps. The round stems normally grow to 1–3 ft (30–90 cm), and they are repeatedly forked, carrying dense whorls of brittle, horn-like foliage, which is dark green in colour with toothed

*Caltha palustris* flore pleno (double marsh marigold)

edges. Floating freely well below the surface, the plant creates a forest of greenery, which is home to a variety of aquatic insects, including mosquito larvae, and it therefore provides a good hunting and breeding ground for fish. It generally sinks to the pool floor on the approach of winter and is propagated by division. It never produces roots.

## Cotula coronopifolia (golden buttons, brass buttons)
This delightful little marginal carpeting plant from the southern hemisphere is for very shallow water. It has smooth creeping stems, 6–12 in (15–30 cm) high, and small, narrow, toothed leaves, $\frac{1}{2}$ in (12 mm) across, which give off a pleasant scent when crushed. It has a very long flowering period, during which it is covered with masses of round, golden flowers like buttons, $\frac{1}{2}$ in (12 mm) in diameter. It is excellent as a marginal plant for pools with shallow edges, growing in up to 5 in (13 cm) of water. Propagation must be by seed sown in spring, as it is usually killed by winter frost.

## Cyperus longus (sweet galingale, English galingale)

A native to Europe, this is a useful hardy marginal plant, which resembles a rush and which, unlike most other members of the genus, will tolerate frosts. It has smooth, three-sided, leafy green stems, 3–4 ft (0.9–1.2 m) high, bearing reddish-brown, arching leafy umbels. It is a delight to the flower arranger and is particularly suitable for the larger pool where it is a good stabilizer of banks where it will vigorously spread from bank to 5 in (13 cm) of water. Herbalists claimed that it could be used for expelling wind and strengthening the bowels; in contrast, the roots have been used in perfumery as an additive to lavender water. Propagation is by division or by seed.

*C. eragrostis (vegetus)* A North American species that is not so tall as *C. longus*, reaching only 2 ft (61 cm) in height. It has reddish-mahogany flowers growing in umbels from the centre of the grass-like leaves, which grow in tufts. Propagation is by division or by seed. Like *C. longus*, it will grow with up to 5 in (13 cm) of water over its crown.

## Dulchium arundinaceum (dwarf bamboo)

An elegant, low, screening or border plant for very damp soil or up to 4 in (10 cm) of water. The $\frac{1}{2}$ in (1 cm) wide, mid-green leaf blades wave gracefully in light wind on stems up to 1 ft 6in (46 cm) tall. It will grow in full or in partial sun. It is a moderate grower only and will not become overly invasive. Propagation is by division.

## Eleocharis (spike rush)

A spiky, grass-like, medium green tufted plant that grows happily in very wet soil or in up to 12 in (31 cm) of water, according to the species. It also grows to a variety of heights. All create an elegant impression in any moisture garden. Propagation is by division.

*E. acicularis (hair grass, needle spike rush)* A native to Europe, Asia and North America, this small submerged oxygenating plant has slender, wiry foliage, 2–12 in (5–30 cm) long, according to the depth of water. It produces numerous runners, which form an underwater carpet. A plant suited to both unheated and tropical aquaria, it is also excellent in tubs or sink gardens.

*E. montevidensis* A tiny, light brown, club-like flowering structure is borne at the top of 1 ft (31 cm) tall, quill-shaped leaves. *E. montevidensis* grows happily in very damp soil or in up to 2 in (5 cm) of water, in full or partial sun.

*E. palustris* Growing in dense tufts, brown spikelets are borne at the top of leafless, 6–12 in (15–31 cm) stems. It grows best in damp soil or in up to 2 in (5 cm) of water.

## Elodea canadensis (Anacharis canadensis) (Canadian pondweed, Babington's curse)

Probably one of the best known submerged oxygenating plants, this native to North America is now naturalized in Europe. It was brought to Ireland in the 1830s and introduced to England 10 years later by a Professor Babington. In England its excessive growth gave it one of its common names. It is now no longer a rampant water weed, seemingly having adjusted to a more reasonable growth rate. The leaves are mid- to dark green, narrow and curving with a pointed tip, up to $\frac{1}{3}$ in (10 mm) long, growing in dense whorls, usually in threes, around the brittle, branching and slender stems. Although it prefers alkaline water, it is otherwise very undemanding and suitable for cold-water aquaria and pools. Although claimed to be invasive, it can be easily held in check by planting it in containers rather than allowing it to romp away in mud at the pool bottom. Aquatic suppliers frequently sell *Elodea crispa*, which is, in fact, *Lagarosiphon major*, and, similarly, if *Elodea densa* is offered, this is, botanically, *Egeria densa*.

## Equisetum (horsetail)

In prehistoric times, gigantic plants of this genus covered many parts of the earth, and the decay of these forests was responsible for the formation of many of our present-day coal deposits. Our current-day *Equisetums* are hollow-stemmed, rush-like, perennial herbs with striking horizontal black bands at each joint of the ribbed, green stem. They grow invasively in damp soil or with up to 6 in (15 cm) of water over their crowns. These plants do not flower, but produce spores from cone-like spikes at the ends of some stems. Propagation is by division or cutting. Ornamental plantings are best with well-restricted root spread.

*E. hyemale (scouring rush)* The most commonly available of the *Equisetums*, this 3 ft (0.9 m) tall plant has been used historically as a cleansing tool. Children enjoy popping the stems apart at its joints.

*E. japonicum* Much like *E. hyemale* culture, this plant has wider, darker black bands at its stem joints, either without or with a whorl of slender branches from each joint. It makes a most dramatic accent plant.

## Eriophorum angustifolium (cotton grass)

This tufted plant has grass-like leaves supporting numerous slender stems of rush-like foliage, 12–15 in (31–38 cm) tall. The main attraction of the plant is the

*Eriophorum angustifolium* (cotton grass)

silky, cotton-wool-like seedheads. Propagation is by seed or division of the rootstock. The plant will grow in very damp soil or in up to 2 in (5 cm) of water.

**Fontinalis antipyretica (willow moss, incombustible water moss)**

A native to Europe, North America and northeast Asia, this attractive little submerged moss has very dark green, narrow leaves, which have no midribs. The leaves tightly clothe the narrow roundish or triangular stems. The specific name, and one of the common names, is associated with its use in Sweden as a fireproofing insulation between walls and chimneys. The generic name also gives a clue to its cultivation – *fontinalis* meaning 'living in fountains'. It grows in cold streams and, like many other small mosses, clings to boulders and wood underwater. It is useful, therefore, to anchor to wood or stones any plants introduced to pools or cold-water aquaria. It must not be planted in

warm water, where it completely degenerates in shallow stagnant ponds. Many forms of tiny aquatic life find refuge among the fronds and so provide food for fish. Propagation is by division.

**Glyceria aquatica variegata (G. spectabilis variegata) (sweet grass, manna grass)**

This beautiful variegated form of the marginal manna grass is native to Europe. It is a vigorous grass, capable of growing in water 3–5 in (8–13 cm) deep, and has stripes of green, yellow and white along the length of the flat leaves, which are 1–2 in (2–5 cm) broad and 2 ft (0.6 cm) tall. The young foliage has a flush of deep rose colour in the spring. It is invasive and should be kept in planting crates. Propagate by division.

**Hottonia palustris (water violet)**

An uncommon plant that is native to Europe. This submerged plant is not a violet but a close relative of the primroses. It spends most of the summer months just below the surface, thrusting the flowers above the water. The much divided leaves are yarrow- or fern-like in whorls of pale green, reaching nearly 5 in (12 cm) long and 3 in (8 cm) wide. Long, white feathery roots can be seen trailing from the leaf joints. The flower arises from the centre of the top leaf whorl and protrudes 6–12 in (15–30 cm) above the water. The arrangement of the flower stem resembles a lady's smock (*Cardamine pratensis*), although the individual flowers resemble those of a primula. The flowers are a pale lavender to white and have a yellow centre. As the flowers fade they submerge and seeds are produced under the water. Winter buds are formed in the autumn, and these also submerge, and the plant disappears until late spring, when it begins life again. If the water is very shallow, the plant forms tufts of long black and slender fibrous roots, which settle into the mud, and it is, therefore tolerant of water from 4 in (10 cm) to 18 in (46 cm) deep. It is a very good oxygenator, and one of the few with attractive flowers. It is not usually available from suppliers until later in the season. When grown outside, it prefers calm and clear water, which does not get too warm.

## Houttuynia

A genus of creeping herbaceous aquatic plants, which are all useful carpeting plants for the pool or stream edge and shallow water. They originate in the Himalayas, China and Japan, and they can be grown in garden borders provided there is adequate moisture, but they are best grown with 0–4 in (0–10 cm) of water over their crowns. They are invasive plants, having creeping rootstocks similar to those of couch grass (*Agropyron repens*).

*H. cordata* The attractive bluish-green, heart-shaped leaves are borne on reddish stems up to 12 in (31 cm) tall, and they make an excellent background for the creamy white flowers, which are supported by four to six white basal bracts. If it is in a sunny position the plant will take on rich autumnal colours. Propagation is by division.

*H. cordata flore pleno* This delightful form develops cone-like centres to the white flowers. It is more restrained than *H. cordata*. The leaves have a strong smell when crushed, some likening it to oranges.

*H. cordata variegata (tricolor)* 'Chameleon' An outstanding variety, which has recently become very popular. The leaves are richly variegated in beautiful shades of cream, crimson and green, and the colours are enhanced in full sunshine.

*Hottonia palustris* (water violet)

### Hydrocharis morsus-ranae (frogbit)

Resembling the tiniest of waterlilies, this floating rootless aquatic is native to Europe and north Asia and a naturalized plant in parts of North America. It is an attractive little floater. The shiny, pale green leaves are thick and leathery but only 1 in (2 cm) across. The small flowers are white with three petals and a yellow centre; male and female flowers are borne on separate plants. It spreads by horizontal stolons, with new plants at the end of the shoots, which later develop oval-shaped resting buds as autumn approaches. These buds drop off and overwinter in mud at the bottom of the pool, rising in early summer to start off new plants. The buds can be kept in water overwinter as a means of propagation. Being a floating plant it is useful as well as decorative in providing shade, which weakens the growth of algae. In shallow water it can get out of hand and should be netted out before this happens. Water snails are fond of its leaves.

### Hypericum elodes (marsh St John's wort)

This water-loving species of the well-known garden Hypericums spreads well in very moist soil or up to 2 in (5 cm) of water to form an attractive mat of woolly, pale-green foliage up to 6 in (15 cm) tall. It bears clusters of

*Iris laevigata* 'Variegata'

Opposite: *Iris kaempferi*

$\frac{1}{2}$ in (1 cm) soft yellow flowers. It is an excellent plant to mask the pool edge. Propagation is by stoloniferous cuttings.

### Iris

A vast genus of which only a few are truly aquatic, their distinctive flowers have erect petals called standards and outer petal-like sepals called falls. The aquatic species are not bearded. When propagating from seed, make sure that the seed is sown fresh.

*I. kaempferi* A really beautiful iris from Japan. The large, clematis-like flowers have horizontal petals, which look like large butterflies and appear in a wide range of colours. Although classed here as an aquatic, it should have only shallow water covering the roots during the summer months, with the plant's crown at least 2 in (5 cm) above water. If the roots are too wet in winter, they will rot. The 2 ft (0.6 m) green, sword-like leaves show a prominent midrib, an important identification aid in distinguishing it from the closely related *I. laevigata*. The falls are about 3 in (8 cm) long, the standards being shorter and narrower. The flower heads are branched, producing two flowers. There are several cultivars with single or double flowers in blue,

purple, pink and white, veined in contrasting colours and broad falls that resemble butterfly wings. They should be planted so that the tops of the roots are 2–3 in (5–8 cm) below the soil and fertilized once a year. Do not plant them in a limy soil. Propagation is by division or by seed.

*I. kaempferi* 'Higo' A remarkable strain of iris, which produces really magnificent clematis-like flowers of enormous size and colour. The delicate and beautiful flowers can measure as much as 10 in (25 cm) across but are remarkably resistant to strong winds. These irises are cultivated in the same way as the species. Propagation is by division in spring.

*I. kaempferi* 'Variegata' This plant has everything, from large, beautiful, clematis-like flowers to delightfully variegated leaves, showing cream and green stripes along their 2 ft (0.6 m) length. It will grow in moist soil only and will not tolerate being grown in the pool. Propagation is by division in spring.

*I. laevigata* Closely related to, and almost identical in appearance with, *I. kaempferi*, this is really one of the finest aquatics for early summer. It comes from Japan and eastern Siberia. The flowers are deep blue, with white or yellow blotches on the fall petals, and they are 4–6 in (10–15 cm) across. The blades of the falls are $2\frac{1}{2}$ in (6 cm) long, and the erect standards are 2 in (5 cm) wide and $2\frac{1}{2}$ in (6 cm) long. The smooth, light green, strap-shaped leaves grow to 2 ft (60 cm) in height and do not have the prominent midrib seen in *I. kaempferi*. This plant is very suitable for a small pool and does well in shallow water, 0–6 in (0–15 cm) deep, or boggy soil, but it must never be allowed to dry out. *I. laevigata* will tolerate lime better than *I. kaempferi*, but it should not be fertilized. The many cultivars may have all white, rose or purple flowers. Propagation is by division in spring or by seed.

*I. laevigata* 'Atropurpurea' A very striking form of iris from Manchuria. The beautiful flowers are almost violet in colour and show up extremely well against the elegant, 2 ft 6 in (76 cm), sword-like leaves. This plant is very suitable for the small pool with 3–5 in (8–13 cm) of water over its crown. Propagation is by division in spring.

*I. laevigata* 'Colchesteri' This beautiful variety has large white flowers, which are heavily mottled with dark blue on the edges of the fall petals. It grows up to 2 ft 6 in (76 cm) tall, with 3–5 in (8–13 cm) of water over its crown. It is very suitable for small pools. Propagation is by division in spring.

*I. laevigata* 'Mottled Beauty' A mottled form, the attractive blue markings show up well against the creamy-white colour of the petals and become more pronounced as the plant matures. Cultivation is as for *I. laevigata*. Propagation is by division in spring.

*I. laevigata* 'Rose Queen' This variety is a hybrid with *I. kaempferi* and is unique in having large, soft, rose-pink flowers and graceful, 2 ft (0.6 m) tall, grass-like foliage. It is at its best in damp soil growing to 2 ft (0.6 m) tall. Propagation is by division in spring.

*I. laevigata* 'Snowdrift' An exceptionally beautiful iris bearing snow-white flowers with pale yellow bases to the petals. Suitable for all types of pool, but especially good in the smaller ones. It grows to 2 ft (0.6 m) tall. Cultivation is as for *I. laevigata*. Propagation is by division in spring.

*I. laevigata* 'Variegata' An exceptionally attractive addition to any pool. As well as producing lavender blue flowers, the 2 ft (0.6 m) leaves have well-defined variegations in green and cream running lengthways, and the whole plant grows in a distinctive fan shape. It is much sought after and consequently can be expensive. The variegated leaves are especially beautiful throughout the summer, doubly so when reflected in dark water. Cultivation is as for *I. laevigata*. Propagation is by division in spring.

*I. pseudacorus* (yellow flag iris) A plant commonly found in marshes and streams all over Europe, Asia Minor and north Africa, even tipping the Arctic Circle. The flower is reputed to be the origin of the *fleur de lis*, when its presence near a bend of the River Rhine reassured King Clovis and the Merovingian army that the river was fordable and so enabled them to escape the forces of the Goths who had trapped them. In gratitude, the flower became the badge of Clovis' successors. Later, Louis VII adopted it as his blazon in the crusades. *Fleur de Louis* became the *Fleur de Luce* and then the *Fleur de lis*.

Although the species is suitable mainly for large pools, some of the cultivars listed below can be grown in smaller pools provided the roots are in a container. Large clusters of yellow flowers, $3–3\frac{1}{2}$ in (8–9 cm) across with roundish falls, $1\frac{1}{4}–1\frac{1}{2}$ in (3–4 cm) wide, are produced with a deeper orange spot at the throat and radiating brown veins. The sword-like leaves are 1 in (2 cm) wide and grow to 3 ft (0.9 m). It looks superb in clumps at the edges of large expanses of water with up

Opposite above: *Iris laevigata* 'Snowdrift'; opposite below: *Iris laevigata* 'Variegata'

to 5 in (13 cm) over its crown. Propagation is by division of the thick rhizomatous roots in early autumn or spring, or from seed.

*I. pseudacorus bastardii* Almost as vigorous as *I. pseudacorus*, this very free-flowering variety has attractive pale cream flowers. It will grow in marshy ground or shallow water. Propagation is by division or seed.

*I. pseudacorus* 'Golden Queen' This form of the native *I. pseudacorus* is slightly more refined and bears large, vivid yellow flowers and a slightly wider leaf. It is not really suitable for small pools. Propagation is by division in spring.

*I. pseudacorus* 'Sulphur Queen' Another plant that is better suited to the larger pool. The large flowers are paler and more primrose yellow than the native yellow flag iris. The sword-like leaves reach about 3 ft (0.9 m) in height. Propagation is by division in spring.

*I. pseudacorus* 'Variegata' A very fine form of *I. pseudacorus* growing up to 2 ft (0.6 m) tall. The attractive leaf variegations in gold and green fade rapidly towards the end of summer. This plant also produces bright golden yellow flowers. Propagation is by division in spring.

*I. versicolor* A native to North America and sometimes described as 'the American laevigata'. Like *I. laevigata* it is as at home in very moist soil as it is in the shallow margins of a pool. It produces attractive and finely shaped violet-blue flowers with conspicuous yellow patches at the base of the petals. The leaves are sword-like and grow to about 2 ft (60 cm) in height. Propagation is by division in spring or by seed in autumn.

*I. versicolor* 'Kermesina' A really beautiful variety, which bears vivid claret-magenta flowers marked with white. This plant grows to about 2 ft (60 cm) in height and is suitable for small pools, being at home in 0–4 in (0–10 cm) of water. Propagation is by division in spring.

### Juncus effusus spiralis (corkscrew rush)
An interesting variety of a large genus of plants known as rushes, they are mainly from temperate regions and are very widespread. Rushes have round, green, pith-filled stems topped with insignificant green or brown flowers in the summer. This particular variety is grown purely for its unusual twisted stems, which grow in a corkscrew fashion to approximately 1 ft 6 in (46 cm) in

Opposite: *Iris pseudacorus* (yellow flag)

height. A talking point in any pool and much sought after by flower arrangers, it grows best with 3–5 in (8–13 cm) of water over its crown. Propagation is by division.

### Lagarosiphon major
A native to South Africa and formerly called *Elodea crispa*, this is one of the most common submerged oxygenating plants, frequently sold by the pet trade in goldfish bowls. The dark-green, pointed and stalkless leaves appear almost whorled in arrangement and are strongly curved, 1 in (2 cm) long, and densely clothe the stems. In water temperatures above 68°F (20°C), the internodes become too long and the plant loses its tight, almost snake-like appearance. It is best planted in groups. The brittle stems and leaves should be cut back periodically, as allowing the overgrown stems to float horizontally on the water is not the best way of showing off the plant.

### Lemna (duckweed)
All of the duckweeds should be treated with great caution as they can easily get out of hand and inhibit the growth of waterlilies and other desirable aquatics, particularly in large or natural pools. In a new pond, where they can be netted out later, there may be a case for their introduction as they can help to cut down light penetration and subsequent algae growth. In the average garden pool, Lemna can serve as an excellent green food for medium-sized to large fish. Four species are distributed worldwide and are commonly seen; all are small, floating plants. They are *L. gibba* (thick duckweed), *L. minor* (common duckweed), *L. polyrrhiza* (greater duckweed) and *L. trisulca* (ivy-leaved duckweed). The last is prettiest of the four, floating just under the water surface, and is an excellent oxygenator.

### Lobelia
The water gardener is concerned with only three or four of the more than 250 species of annual and perennial lobelias.

*L. cardinalis* (cardinal flower) This eye-catching North American plant has tapering spikes of vivid scarlet, salvia-like flowers and reddish-bronze foliage. It is usually grown as a border plant needing some protection, but in milder districts it is possible to grow it in water 3–4 in (8–10 cm) deep, and it will make a striking waterside plant. Propagation is by division, seeds or cuttings. *L. fulgens* is a similar species but has plain green foliage.

*L. dortmanna* (water lobelia) A submerged oxygenator from Europe and North America, the water lobelia has a

*Lysichitum americanum*

carpeting habit, with rosettes of dark-green ribbon-shaped leaves, 4 in (10 cm) long and $\frac{1}{5}$ in (4–5 mm) wide. The leaves are blunt at the ends and frequently arched. In shallow water, the pale lavender, bell-shaped flowers, which have white bands, appear above the surface.

## Lysichitum (skunk cabbage)
A genus requiring conditions bordering between marsh and very damp soil. Both species are successful as marginal plants if there is ample deep, rich soil and space to show off their huge architectural leaves. They have thickly clustered flower stems with huge spathes, which look beautiful when reflected in the water. They do, however, take time to become established and resent transplanting.

*L. americanum* A very handsome North American plant bearing large, deep-yellow flowers, 12 in (30 cm) high, which are arum-lily shaped and have a thick, parchment-like texture. They appear before the large pointed green leaves, which can reach 3 ft (0.9 m) in height, in the early spring. This plant has considerable architectural merit. Propagation is by division, seed and self-set seedlings.

*L. camschatcense* This Japanese plant has very attractive, pure white, almost translucent, flowers which are arum-lily like in shape. The leaves are large, up to 3 ft (0.9 m) tall, green and pointed. A beautiful plant for wet soil and certainly one to be recommended for an informal pool margin. Propagation is by division or self-set seedlings.

## Mentha aquatica (water mint)
A native north European plant. It is vigorous and has strongly aromatic, oval, hairy and toothed leaves, 1–2$\frac{1}{2}$ in (2–6 cm) across, which are almost obscured in late summer by clustered 9 in (23 cm) spikes of pale lavender flowers, to which bees are known to be attracted. The plant frequently appears of its own accord, and because, like other mints, it has a creeping rootstock, it should be kept in a container to prevent it wandering all over the shallow edges of a pool. It will grow in moving water. Plant it where disturbance of the leaves is likely in order to take advantage of the scent. Propagation is by division, cuttings or seed.

## Menyanthes trifoliata (bog bean)
A native to northern temperate regions, this is an extremely useful plant for hiding the edges of artificial pools because of its scrambling habit. The leaves, which are broad-bean-like and grow in threes on a single stem,

are 1–3 in (2–8 cm) across. They are one of the food plants of the elephant hawk moth larvae. In early spring the attractive white flowers, which are $\frac{1}{2}$ in (12 mm) across and have purple stamens and a pink fringe to the petals, appear on spikes from pink buds. It grows up to 9 in (23 cm) in height in water 2–4 in (5–10 cm) deep. Propagation is by division.

## Mimulus (monkey flower)

A very showy genus of moisture-loving annuals and perennials, which form spreading masses of light green foliage and brilliant antirrhinum-shaped flowers. They may not survive severe winters so must be protected or renewed most years. They have a wide range of tolerance of most soil types and may meander happily into the water and grow on the submerged marginal shelves as well as being at home in the drier conditions on a bank.

*M. luteus* (monkey musk, water musk) Native to Chile, this plant has naturalized itself throughout Britain and

produces colour when the main burst of summer aquatic flowers are over. The plant has hollow stems, 4–18 in (10–46 cm) high, with close tufts of hairy foliage bearing an abundance of bright yellow flowers, $\frac{3}{4}$–2 in (2–5 cm) long, with two dark marks at the mouth and speckled with red. The leaf edges are serrated and light green in colour. The plant makes quite an impact when planted in clumps in shallow water 0–2 in (0–5 cm) deep. Propagation is by division, seed or cuttings.

*M. ringens* (lavender musk) A native to eastern North America, this is a truly aquatic musk, which prefers shallow water, 3–5 in (8–13 cm) deep. It has tall, erect, square, much branched stems, which are 1–3 ft (30–90 cm) high. The mainly stalkless leaves are longer, narrower and darker green than those of *M. luteus*. The flowers are a delicate blue or bluish-violet, 1–1½ in (2–3 cm) long, with two lips and a narrow throat. Fresh vigour is given to the plant when it is regularly

*Mimulus luteus* (monkey musk)

propagated by cuttings. An attractive addition to any pool. Propagation is by division, seed or cuttings.

## Myosotis scorpioides (M. palustris) (water forget-me-not)

A European native, this is an ideal plant for the pool edge with its oblong, bright-green, hairy leaves and intensely bright blue flowers, about $\frac{1}{3}$ in (8 mm) across, with yellow or pink eyes. It seeds itself into lovely drifts of blue and will even thrive in shade. It will often produce long floating stems, which trail out into the water. It will grow up to 10 in (2 cm) high in 0–3 in (0–8 cm) of water. Propagation is by seed or cutting.

## Myriophyllum vertillicatum (water milfoil)

A submerged oxygenator from Europe, Asia, North Africa and North America, this attractive plant has stems up to 6 ft 6 in (2 m) long, bearing crowded whorls of bright green leaves, 1–2 in (2–5 cm) long and cut into thread-like segments. This delicate filigree foliage makes an excellent area for fish eggs. Removing the growing tips for cuttings encourages the new side-shoots to appear. It likes acid water.

## Nuphar (yellow pond lily)

This genus contains plants that are similar to waterlilies but that thrive in deeper and colder water, even in moving water. They have long, creeping rhizomatous rootstocks, which are 4 in (10 cm) thick and can grow to 6 ft (1.8 m) long, with prominent scars left by the old leaf stalks. They have two types of leaves – the attractive submerged leaves, which are thin and translucent and resemble underwater ferns, and the floating leaves, which are oval, thick and leathery and have heart-shaped bases. When the plant becomes overcrowded, the floating leaves are often thrust above the water. The yellow flowers are 2 in (5 cm) in diameter, with five sepals (N. advena is an exception with six sepals) and many petals, resembling stamens, surrounding an aromatic bottle-shaped fruit, which gives the plant one of its common names, brandy bottle. They will grow in a variety of water depths and in partial shade, and they are a useful alternative in situations that are unsuitable for waterlilies. The large seed pods of the cow lily (N. polysepala) were collected in boats by the North American Kalamath Indians and later roasted into a form of popcorn on hot griddles or ground into a mealy substitute for flour. Propagation and cultivation is the same as for waterlilies.

N. advena (American spatterdock, common spatterdock, mooseroot) Native to the eastern United States, this is one of the most common and better species, particularly for shady sites. The globular flowers, with their bright coppery red stamens, are 2–3½ in (5–9 cm) in diameter with six sepals, the three outer ones a dirty yellow, the inner three a golden colour. The oval leaves, 4–11 in (10–28 cm) long and 5–9 in (13–23 cm) wide, are floating, sometimes erect above the water near the crown. It will tolerate a great variety of water depths.

N. japonica rubrotinctum (Japanese pond lily) This Japanese species has large, arrow-shaped, dark olive green, curled foliage, 4–10 in (10–25 cm) long, and large cup-shaped orange-scarlet flowers. It prefers still water and is somewhat rare.

N. lutea (yellow pond lily, brandy bottle) A native to Europe, including the British Isles, and to north Asia, this species produces masses of leathery-green heart-shaped leaves, 16 in (41 cm) long and 12 in (30 cm) wide, with alcoholic-smelling, bottle-shaped bright yellow flowers. It will grow well in running or deep water. The rhizomatous roots have been used for tanning and in Sweden for a form of bread.

N. pumila (minima) A native to Europe and north Asia, this species has smaller leaves. They are heart-shaped and deeply cut but 5 in (13 cm) across, which makes it more suitable for the garden pool where it will grow in 12 in (30 cm) of water and be less invasive than the other species. It has tiny yellow flowers.

## Nymphoides peltata (Nymphoides peltata var. Bennettii, Villarsia Bennettii) (water fringe, floating heart)

The only hardy species of this genus that is native to Europe and Asia and that has also become naturalized in North America. A small floating plant for shallow water 6–18 in (15–46 cm) deep, it resembles a miniature waterlily with its rounded, bright green leaves mottled in brown, 2 in (5 cm) in diameter. The dainty yellow flowers with fringed petals are 1 in (2 cm) across and produced in clusters held about 2 in (5 cm) above the surface of the water. It can be extremely invasive, particularly in shallow water where the long trailing stems take root as they travel, but it can be useful for giving surface cover while waterlilies are becoming established. It should be kept in check before it gets out of hand. Propagation is by seed or division.

## Orontium aquaticum (golden club)

A North American plant with large, velvety, dark green leaves with a silvery metallic sheen. It can grow in

Opposite above: Myriophyllum vertillicatum (water milfoil); opposite below: Orontium aquaticum (golden club)

*Pontederia cordata* (pickerel weed)

under 12 in (30 cm) of water, where it produces floating leaves, 5–12 in (13–30 cm) long and 5 in (13 cm) wide, or it can grow in shallow water, where it produces much larger bluish-green leaves on 18 in (46 cm) stems. The white, pencil-like flowers are tipped with yellow, like the interior of a calla lily with its golden pokers. It should be started in a large planting crate in shallow water and later moved into deeper water as it becomes established. The plant has a deep root system and is very difficult to transplant. Propagation is by well ripened seed or division.

### Peltandra (arrow arums)

These North American marginal plants, closely related to the arums, have large, dark green, glossy, arrow-shaped leaves, 14 in (36 cm) long and 8 in (20 cm) wide. They have arum-like flowers, 3–4 in (8–10 cm) long, in mid-spring. They are best grown in clumps and propagated by seed or division.

*P. alba sagittifolia* This species has firm, strongly veined, bright green arrow-shaped leaves and white flowers, 18 in (46 cm) tall, that later produce red berries.

*P. virginiana* Growing to a height of 2 ft (60 cm), this species has green flowers followed by green berries.

### Pontederia

These are excellent, robust plants that grow in very wet mud or with up to 5 in (13 cm) of water over their crowns.

*P. cordata* (pickerel weed) A common marginal plant in North America, where it grows wild in rivers and streams. It owes its common name to young pike, which enjoy hiding among the stems. It is one of the easiest and most beautiful of marginal aquatics for any type of pool, with its neat growth of superb, glossy, heart-shaped leaves on smooth, rounded stems, 2 ft (60 cm) high. The soft blue flowers grow as spikes, 6 in (15 cm) in length, and are produced from summer through to autumn, making it invaluable in providing flower when most marginals are past their best. Having a vigorous creeping rhizome, it is best planted in a large container of heavy loam to keep it in check. Propagation is by division or seed. *P. azurea* is much the same as *P. cordata* but has purple-blue flower spires.

*P. lanceolata (P. angustifolia)* Very distinct from *P. cordata*, this plant has narrow, dark green foliage and deep blue flower spikes. The entire plant can reach up to 4 ft (1.2 m) in height. It is grown under the same conditions as *P. cordata*.

## Potamogeton (pondweed)
It may be useful to include a few species of this rampant, submerged and native water weed in large pools where fish and waterfowl, particularly swans, are considered a priority. They are all good oxygenators but very difficult to maintain. The species with floating leaves are very decorative when young but rapidly outgrow their space in a small pool. They have two types of leaves – floating and submerged. The following two species have submerged leaves only, which are the only types to consider, even in very large pools.

*P. crispus* (curled pondweed) This species, which is widely distributed, has oblong, wavy-edged and tapering submerged leaves; they are bronze-green and translucent. The flowers are brown and borne in short spikes.

*P. pectinatus* (fennel-leaved pondweed) A native to Europe and Australia, this species is often found in brackish water, where its finely divided leaves grow in dense masses.

## Potentilla palustris (Comarum palustris) (bog strawberry, purple cinquefoil, marsh cinquefoil)
This moisture-loving species of *Potentilla* produces 1 ft (31 cm) tall mounds of strawberry-like leaves and 1 in (3 cm) reddish-purple flowers. It is propagated by division of stolons.

## Ranunculus
An interesting perennial plant adapted to a variety of pool conditions.

*R. aquatilis* (water crowfoot, water buttercup) A common submerged species with a wide temperate distribution, including Europe and North America. One of the prettiest native plants, it grows in great profusion in slow-moving rivers although preferring stagnant waters, where it forms large colonies. There are two types of leaves – submerged and floating. The sub-

merged leaves are limp and delicate, shrivelling quickly as soon as they are removed from water, and finely dissected into numerous segments. The floating leaves, on the other hand, are kidney-shaped and lobed at the base of the leaf blades. It tends to become invasive, growing quickly into dense spreading masses, which, in spring, are covered in myriads of snow-white buttercup-like flowers with yellow centres held above the water surface. Another native species, *R. circinalis* (*divaricatus*), the rigid-leaved crowfoot, has only round submerged foliage on long leafy stems, and these do not shrivel when taken out of the water.

*R. flammula* (lesser spearwort) A smaller and less showy plant than *R. lingua*, it is more suitable for the smaller pool. It grows to 12 in (31 cm) in damp soil or up to 3 in (8 cm) of water. The flowers are not so large and have pale yellow, glossy petals. Propagation is by division, seed or cuttings.

*R. lingua* (spearwort) Native to Europe and temperate Asia, this is a good marginal plant for the larger pool. It grows to about 3 ft (90 cm) in height and has thick, deep pink hollow stems and lance-shaped leaves, 8 in (20 cm) long and $\frac{3}{4}$–1 in (15–20 mm) wide. Submerged leaves form in the winter and early spring only. The plant grows best with 3–6 in (8–15 cm) of water over its crown. The flowers, which are held on branching stems, are a glistening golden colour, similar to, but, at 2 in (5 cm) across, much larger than those of a buttercup. Although claimed to be invasive, it is not too difficult to keep in check. The form *grandiflora* has larger flowers. Propagation is by division or seed.

## Sagittaria (arrowhead)
Known as arrowheads, these handsome but rampant marginals have a worldwide distribution with a hardy species that is native to Britain. They reproduce themselves by small tubers, division or seed. The tubers are attractive to ducks and have given the plants popular names such as 'duck potato' and 'swamp potato'; some sort of protection may be required if ducks are present. The tubers are the overwintering organs that develop on the ends of runners as the plant dies down in the autumn. In the spring, runner-like shoots develop from the tips of the tubers and eventually form new leaves. They all grow best with 3–5 in (8–13 cm) of water over their crowns.

*S. sagittifolia* (common arrowhead) A species from north Europe. It has beautiful, acutely arrow-shaped, shiny leaves, which are held above the water on succulent stems, 15–18 in (38–46 cm) tall. The white flowers are 1 in (2 cm) in diameter and have conspicuous black and

*Sagittaria japonica* 'Flore Pleno'

*Saururus cernuus* (swamp lily)

crimson centres. The species develops three types of leaves: submerged leaves, which are long and develop only when sprouting in the spring; floating leaves, which are oval; and aerial leaves, which are arrow-shaped. If the plant is growing in running water the aerial leaves adapt to a more strap-shaped, floating form. Although suitable for all types of pool, it needs to be kept under control by planting into containers. Propagation is by division or seed.

*S. japonica* (*S. variabilis*) Very similar to *S. sagittifolia* but producing leaves that are broader arrows and taller, up to 2 ft 6 in (76 cm), with red stem-bases. The flowers have bright yellow centres.

*S. japonica* 'Flore pleno' An extremely attractive form of Sagittaria, having not only the thrusting, 18 in (46 cm) tall, arrow-shaped leaves, but also such full petals that the yellow centres on which the double snow-white flowers grow are nearly obscured. Propagation is by division or from tubers.

*Scirpus lacustris* 'Albescens'

*S. latifolia* (duck potato) This plant grows much taller than *S. japonica* and can easily exceed 3 ft (0.9 m). The flowers are similar to the other arrowheads.

**Saururus cernuus (swamp lily, lizard's tail, water dragon)**

A North American plant, the common name refers to the shape of the flower. The long spikes of fragrant white flowers are pendulous and up to 6 in (15 cm) long. In autumn the heart-shaped leaves, which are 6 in (15 cm) long and 2–3 in (5–8 cm) wide, take on rich autumnal tints and produce an interesting scent when crushed. The entire plant can reach 2 ft (0.6 m) in height in damp soil or up to 2 in (5 cm) of water. Propagation is by division or cuttings.

**Scirpus**

A large genus with worldwide distribution, they are the true bulrushes, which have been used commercially for chairmaking and mattresses. They are generally too large for very small gardens. They have masses of minute brown flowers. All grow well with 3–5 in (8–13 cm) of water over the crown.

*S. lacustris* A European native with tall, dark-green, cylindrical stems, 3–8 ft (0.9–2.4 m) high, bearing tiny hanging tassels of reddish-brown flowers. It is useful as a single specimen in a wildlife garden if height is required in the planting scheme.

*S. lacustris* subsp. *tabernaemontani* Similar to *S. lacustris* but with more substantial, steely blue foliage. It has an attractive mealy bloom.

*S. lacustris* subsp. *tabernaemontani* 'Albescens' A European species that makes an attractive, 3–5 ft (0.9–1.5 m), architectural plant, with round, rushy stems vertically lined with green and cream. It is best grown in a container to prevent excessive spreading. Propagation is by division.

*S. lacustris* subsp. *tabernaemontani* 'Zebrinus' (zebra rush) Originating in Japan, this species has striking foliage, 1–3 ft (30–90 cm) tall, the fine, rush-like leaves alternately banded with green and white rather like porcupine quills. A very distinctive addition to the pool. Propagation is by division.

### Sparganium erectum (S. ramosum) (burr reed)

Native to Europe and North America, this is one of the larger aquatic plants. The attractive leaves, 2 ft 6 in–4 ft (0.8–1.2 m) tall, are triangular at the base, terminating in a sharp point. The branched flower head produces round spiky flowers and fruits. Growing in 3–5 in (8–13 cm) of water, the plant looks very attractive when young. However, it must be introduced into an artificial pond with great caution as it not only spreads very rapidly but it can also easily puncture liners with the needle-sharp growing tips on the underground rhizomes. It should therefore be restricted to a rigid container or introduced to large pools for wildlife cover only. Propagation is by division or seed.

### Stratiotes aloides (water soldier, water cactus)

An unusual floating plant of European origin. The rosettes of leaves, 2–8 in (5–20 cm) long, are spiny and

*Stratiodes aloides* (water soldiers)

resemble the top of a pineapple. It floats just under the water until about mid-summer, when the three-petalled flowers appear. These are snow-white, about 1 in (2 cm) across, and the male and female flowers are borne on separate plants. The male flowers are in clusters in a pink, papery spathe, while the females are produced singly in the axis of the leaves. Generally, plants of one sex tend to be found, so that reproduction is more likely to be through vegetative means than seed. After flowering, the plant sinks to the bottom and comes to the surface again in August or later. Meanwhile, at the bottom of the pond, shoots bearing large buds are produced, and on the plant's return to the surface in August, these grow into young plants. They break free, sink to the bottom and remain there for the winter. The young plants look quite attractive. It is a good oxygenating plant but should be introduced with care into pools where it can spread very rapidly. Its sale and shipment in the United States is restricted because of this tendency.

### Tillaea recurva (Crassula helmsii)

A native to Australia and New Zealand, this is a creeping evergreen submerged plant with hard, cress-like foliage. It is a good oxygenator all the year round

and can be grown in a wide range of situations from aquaria to shallow water or wet mud. The branching stems, which can grow to 3 ft (90 cm) are packed with small, needle-like, fleshy leaves $\frac{1}{6}$ in (4 mm) long, which can float on the water's surface. The insignificant white flowers appear near the tops of the stems in summer. It can be extremely invasive so must be used only in situations where its spread will not cause problems later. It is not, therefore, recommended for natural pools. Propagation is by cuttings or division.

## Typha (reedmace, cat's-tail)

These common marginal plants, with a worldwide distribution, are often erroneously referred to as bulrushes. They are extremely invasive and great care must be taken with their introduction to small areas. They have rootstocks with sharp points, which could easily damage a liner. The long poker-like flowers are a familiar sight in native pools and much sought after by flower arrangers.

*T. angustifolia* (lesser reedmace) Native to Europe, west Asia, North America, Australia and north Africa, this is a rather stately plant with graceful, grey-green leaves, $\frac{1}{2}$ in (12 mm) wide and 6 ft (1.8 m) tall, and chocolate-brown, poker-like fruiting heads. The male flowers, which sit higher on the stem than the female, are separated by approximately 1 in (2 cm) of stem. It should be grown in a container as it is rather invasive, and is only suitable for large pools. It grows in mud or in up to 6 in (15 cm) of water. It makes a more graceful plant than the more common *T. latifolia*. Propagation is by division.

*T. latifolia* (great reedmace) Native to Europe, Asia and North America, this is the species most commonly referred to as the common bulrush. It has been used for making mats and baskets, and the floss from the seed heads is used as a filling for cushions and pillows. It is the giant of the family, growing to 8 ft (2.4 m) in height, and it is out of scale except in really large water gardens. It produces large, flat, grassy-like leaves, 1 in (2 cm) wide, which are grey-green in colour, and thick poker-heads of flowers. Even when contained, the rhizomatous root is capable of growing over concrete walls. They thrive in 3–5 in (8–13 cm) of water. Propagation is by division or seed.

*T. laxmanii* (*stenophylla*) (small reedmace) A native to Europe, Asia and North America, this is a very much more restrained Typha, growing little more than 3 ft (90 cm) high and producing slender, willowy leaves and

Opposite: *Typha latifolia*

*Typha laxmanii* (small reedmace)

*Typha minima* (miniature reedmace)

attractive dark brown pokers. It will grow in mud or in up to 6 in (15 cm) of water. Propagation is by division or seed.

*T. minima* (miniature reedmace) A native to Europe, Asia and North America, this is a really delightful, dwarf species with delicate reed-like leaves, 18 in (46 cm) tall, bluish-green in colour. The short, round pokers are extremely attractive. It is really the only suitable reedmace for small to medium pools, growing in mud or up to 4 in (10 cm) of water. Propagation is by division or seed.

### Utricularia vulgaris

One of the few hardy species of a genus that is mainly found in tropical waters. It is an unusual submerged aquatic, which is also carnivorous. The stems form a tangled mass, 6–18 in (15–46 cm) across, of attractive, hair-like leaves, $\frac{3}{4}$–1 in (2 cm) long, similar to a Myriophyllum, but covered in minute dark green to brown dot-like bladders. It remains submerged until ready to flower, when the tiny bladders, which are hidden in the foliage, become inflated and bring the plant to the surface. The flowers, which are held

sparsely on spikes, resemble small snapdragon flowers. They are a rich golden yellow with orange tips and are $\frac{1}{2}$–$\frac{3}{4}$ in (12–19 mm) long. After flowering, the bladders fill with water and sink again. The plant absorbs dissolved minerals from the water directly into its foliage, but the carnivorous bladders suck microscopic aquatic animals in through trap-doors, triggered by hairy growths at their entrance. Winter buds form, and these also sink to the bottom and restart into growth in the spring.

### Veronica beccabunga (brooklime)

The sprawling habit of this native to Europe, Asia and north Africa, makes this an excellent plant for the pool's edge, where it grows up to 12 in (31 cm). The succulent creeping stems, which sprawl in all directions, bear almost evergreen, dark green leaves. The clusters of small bright blue flowers, $\frac{1}{3}$ in (8 mm) across, are similar to forget-me-nots and have conspicuous white eyes. They are produced in abundance throughout the summer. It is somewhat invasive, requiring thinning, and should be cut back when it becomes lanky after seeding. Propagation is by division, seed or cuttings. The plant can grow in slowly running water.

# GARDENS TO VISIT

## British Water Gardens

Gardens combining good presentation with a reasonable variety of species or hybrids, particularly gardens that have labels to help with identification, are not common in Britain. There are several gardens with a few waterlilies, but very often not only is the variety not known but the cultivation also leaves a lot to be desired.

The finest collections of hardy waterlilies can be found at Burnby Hall Gardens in Pocklington, Humberside, where there are approaching 50 varieties, all of which are labelled, in the two lakes. Stapeley Water Gardens maintains this collection, which was started by Major P. M. Stewart in the early 1930s when the lakes were altered for more decorative use than trout fishing. There are over 20 varieties in the larger upper pool, including an excellent stand of 'James Brydon', a brilliant red variety that displays hundreds of flowers each day in mid-summer. The smaller lower lake contains upwards of a dozen varieties. The attention given to thinning out is evident, as most of the leaves sit beautifully on the surface and are not spoilt by overcrowding. Major Stewart gave the garden to Pocklington in trust in 1962. It is situated 11 miles east of York off the A1079 where one turns east on to the B1246. It is open from Easter until the end of September, on Mondays to Fridays from 10.00 a.m. to 7.00 p.m and on Saturdays and Sundays from noon to 7.00 p.m.

Lakes at different levels are also the setting of another fine show of waterlilies at Sheffield Park in east Sussex. The gardens, which are under the skilful management of the National Trust, are better known for the trees than the waterlilies. Chiefly a garden to be enjoyed for spring or autumn colour, the well-maintained waterlilies provide quite a spectacle on the large lakes, which are framed by, and which themselves reflect, some beautiful conifers. Sheffield Park is 10 miles north of Lewes on the A275. It is open from April until mid-November, on Tuesdays to Saturdays (except the Tuesday after a Bank Holiday Monday and on Good Friday) from 11.00 a.m. to 6.00 p.m. and on Sundays and Bank Holiday Mondays from 2.00 to 6.00 p.m.

Developed by three generations of the Aberconway family since 1874, Bodnant Garden is not only one of the finest gardens in the country but has an excellent show of waterlilies on the second terrace below the house. The majority of the waterlilies can be seen near a beautiful cedar on this terrace, but another long, formal pool on the Canal Terrace houses some good groups at either end. Bodnant is 8 miles south of Colwyn Bay on the A470, the entrance being on the road to Eglwysbach. It is open from mid-March until the end of October, from 10.00 a.m. to 5.00 p.m.

Any visit to Cheshire should include a stop at Stapeley Water Gardens, which displays the largest collection in the world of hardy waterlilies. Over 100 different varieties are grown in an extensive park-like setting, where any of the waterlilies and all water gardening supplies may be bought. The Palms Tropical Oasis, a 1-acre conservatory garden, houses a vast collection of day- and night-blooming tropical and Victoria waterlilies. Stapeley Water Gardens is located 1 mile south of Nantwich on the A51, 10 minutes from Junction 16 on the M6. The Gardens are open all year round, seven days a week (except Christmas Day). During the summer it is open from 10.00 a.m. to 7.00 p.m. at weekends and on Bank Holidays, and from 9.00 a.m. to 6.00 p.m. on week days; during the winter it is open from 10.00 a.m. to 5.00 p.m. at weekends and from 9.00 a.m. to 5.00 p.m. on week days.

The Royal Horticultural Society's Garden at Wisley has a fairly recently planted collection in the formal pool in front of the laboratory building seen on entering. As might be expected for such a famous garden, there are also many other good collections of marginals and deep floating aquatics. Wisley is 7 miles east of Guildford in Surrey and may be reached by turning off the A3. It is open from Monday to Saturday from 10.00 a.m. to 7.00 p.m. and Sundays from 2.00 to 7.00 p.m. (Check with the Society, as Sundays are restricted to members only.)

Kew Gardens in Richmond, Surrey, has a collection of waterlilies and aquatics, and the glasshouse range allows more tropical species, including *Victoria regia*, to be displayed than the average garden collection. Kew is situated on the A307 at Kew Bridge, $\frac{1}{4}$ mile west of Kew Gardens Station. It is open daily, excluding Christmas Day and New Year's Day, from 10.00 am until dusk.

Another superb collection of waterlilies and aquatic plants may be seen at Longstock Gardens near Stockbridge in Hampshire. These gardens are owned by the John Lewis Partnership and open to the public on only a few Sunday afternoons in aid of charity. The Water Gardens, which were planned with the help of the famous Perry's Hardy Plant Farm in the 1950s, form only one part of a very large and beautiful estate, which has a small nursery full of aquatic and moisture-loving treasures. The Water Gardens form a series of lush lagoons created by inlets of the River Test. It is the ultimate in water gardening – beautiful waterlilies are surrounded by sensitive planting at the water's edge. Longstock is about 3 miles north of Stockbridge; turn off the A30 in Stockbridge. The Water Gardens are normally open on the third Sunday of each month from April to September between 2.00 and 6.00 pm, but it would be advisable to check first.

While in Hampshire, it is not too far to visit Compton Acres in Poole, Dorset. These famous gardens have several theme gardens dominated by water, and water-lilies may be seen in a variety of settings. The Italian Garden, with its cross-shaped pool, contains a selection of varieties that are displayed with particularly good effect. The gardens are 2 miles west of Bournemouth on the A35; turn south to Canford Cliffs. They are open from April to the end of October, from 10.30 a.m. to 6.30 p.m.

## American Water Gardens

It would seem natural that the home of the famous hybridist George Pring would have a good collection, and this is certainly the case. The lilies are housed in the Missouri Botanical Gardens in St Louis, and the tropical varieties provide a riot of colour in some very dramatic

Opposite: Burnby Hall Gardens at Pocklington, Humberside, have one of the best collections of waterlilies to be seen in the UK

settings. Similarly, Longwood Gardens 30 miles west of Philadelphia in the historic Brandywine Valley near Kennett Square, Pennsylvania, leaves breathtaking memories of waterlilies large and small. Longwood has hybridized its own Victoria hybrid, and the pools between the conservatories have dramatic plantings of aquatics including some interesting canna hybrids, again developed at Longwood.

Joe Tomocik maintains a superb collection of hardy and tropical waterlilies and other aquatic plants at the Denver Botanic Garden in Colorado, where the beautiful display pools are artfully blended with the other specialty collections.

As in Britain, there are many nurseries where varieties can be seen without a garden setting. In America a collection of lotus and waterlilies can be seen at Perry's Water Gardens, 8 miles north-west of Franklin, N. C. This nursery must be mentioned as one of the best collections of hardy waterlilies to be seen in the United States. The beautiful setting of the Cowee Valley seems to intensify the flower colours. Undoubtedly, the combination of climate, soil and care from Perry Slocum and Ben Gibson shows how waterlilies should be grown.

# USEFUL ADDRESSES

International Water Lily Society
P.O. Box 104
Buskeystown
Maryland 21717-0104
U.S.A.

International Water Lily Society
Wycliffe Hall Botanical Gardens
Barnard Castle
County Durham DL12 9TS
U.K.

Royal Horticultural Society
P.O. Box 313
Vincent Square
London SW1P 2PE
U.K.

# GLOSSARY

**Anther** The part of the stamen collecting the pollen grain

**Cordate** Heart-shaped

**Crown** Upper part of fleshy or woody rootstock from which shoots arise

**Filament** The stalk of a stamen

**Genus** Group of species with common characteristics

**Inflorescence** The arrangement of flowers on the flower stalk

**Hybrid** Plant produced by fertilization of one species by another

**Lanceolate** Tapered towards each end with the broadest point below the middle

**Marginal** Aquatic plants whose roots like to grow in shallow water around the pool's edge

**Node** A joint in the stem from which a leaf springs

**Peltate** With the stalk attached to the centre of a leaf

**Petiole** A leaf stalk

**Raceme** Arrangement of a flower, as in bluebells, where there is an elongated central axis with flowers carried separately along its length, each on its own flower stalk

**Reflexed** Tips of petals or sepals that bend back

**Rhizome** A storage organ that is really a modified stem and capable of producing roots and shoots; it normally progresses horizontally and may be below ground or level with the surface

**Rosette** A cluster of leaves, densely packed together in a wheel-like form, often flat on the ground but sometimes partially upright

**Runner** A rooting stem produced at soil level and forming a new plant that eventually becomes detached from the parent

**Sinus** Depression between two lobes or teeth

**Spadix** The thick, fleshy, pencil-like organ of an arum 'flower', which carries many very small male and female flowers near the base

**Spathe** A modified, usually papery, leaf, which encloses the whole flower cluster in the bud stage; in Callas, Lysichitums and other Arums it is the most conspicuous part of the 'flower'

**Species** The specific plant within a genus

**Spike** A raceme in which the individual flowers have no stalks; it is thus a very dense inflorescence

**Stamen** The male portion of the flower; it produces pollen and consists of the filament (stalk) and anther (pollen-bearing part)

**Stellate** Star-shaped

**Stolon** A creeping stem produced at soil level

**Tuber** A swollen underground stem that is solid, unlike a bulb, which is scaly

**Umbel** A type of inflorescence in which all the flowers arise from the same point at the apex of the stem, like the spokes of an umbrella, as in the case of butomus, the flowering rush

**Viviparous** Producing young plants vegetatively from the leaf of the original plant

**Whorl** Leaves or flowers, all of which arise from the same point on a stem or circle around it, as in candelabra primulas

# BIBLIOGRAPHY

Allgayo and Titon, *The Complete Book of Aquarium Plants*, Ward Lock, 1987

Heritage, W., *Ponds and Water Gardens*, Blandford Press, 1981

Masters, C. D., *Encyclopedia of the Water Lily*, T.F.H. Publications Ltd, 1974

Mühlberg, H., *The Complete Guide to Water Plants*, E.P. Publishing Ltd, 1982

Perry, Frances, *The Water Garden*, Ward Lock, 1981

Russell, Stanley, *The Stapeley Book of Water Gardens*, David & Charles, 1985

Stodola, J., *Encyclopedia of Water Plants*, T.F.H. Publications Ltd, 1967

Swindells, Philip, *Waterlilies*, Croom Helm Ltd, 1983

Bodnant Gardens have a fine formal pool with excellent groups of waterlilies

# INDEX

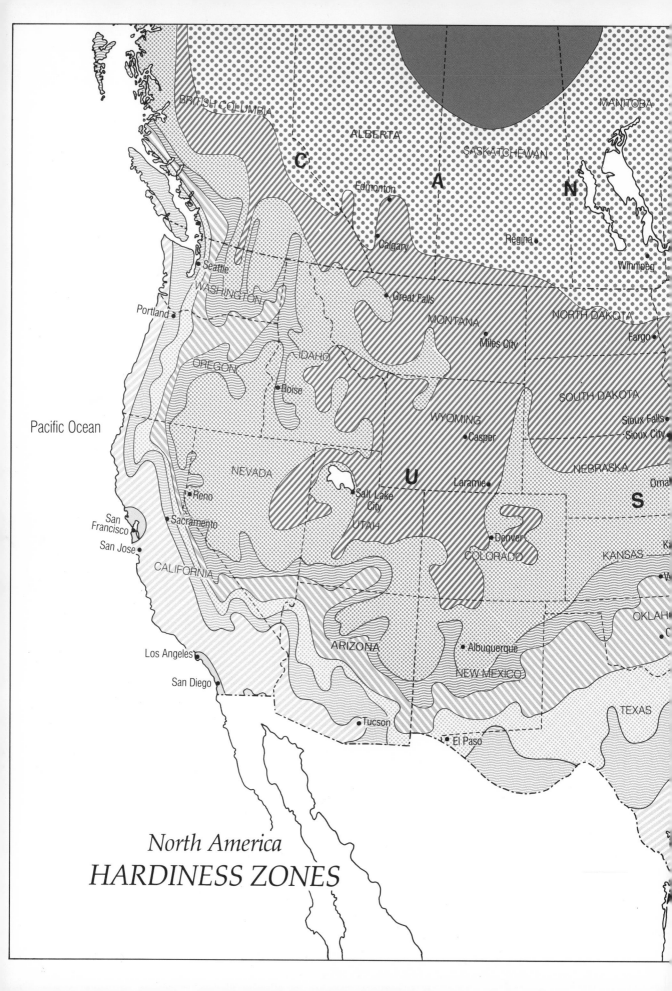

*North America*
## HARDINESS ZONES